GAINING A MASTER'S DEGREE

How To Books for Students

Budgeting for Students
Critical Thinking for Students
Gaining a Master's Degree
Getting a Job after University
Going to University
How to Know Your Rights: Students
How to Know Your Rights: Teachers
How to Master GCSE Accounts
How to Master Languages
How to Pass Exams Without Anxiety
How to Start Word Processing
How to Study Abroad
How to Study & Learn
How to Study & Live in Britain
How to Survive at College
How to Teach Abroad
How to Use a Library

How to Write a Report
Improving Your Written English
Mastering Book-keeping
Mastering Business English
Passing That Interview
Planning Your Gap Year
Research Methods
Spending a Year Abroad
Studying at University
Studying for a Degree
Taking in Students
Taking Your A-Levels
Writing an Assignment
Writing an Essay
Writing Business Letters
Writing Your Dissertation

Further titles in preparation

The How To series now contains more than 200 titles in the
following categories:

Business Basics
Family Reference
Jobs & Careers
Living & Working Abroad
Media Skills

Mind & Body
New Technology
Student Handbooks
Successful Writing
Travel

Please send for a free copy of the latest catalogue for full details
(see back cover for address).

STUDENT HANDBOOKS

GAINING A
MASTER'S DEGREE

How to invest in your own future

Dr Allen Brown

ONE DAY SON, ALL THIS WILL
BE YOURS ... AS SOON AS YOU
GET YOUR DEGREE!

How To Books

Dedication

To the memory of my mother,
Mrs Mary Jane Brown

British Library Cataloguing-in-Publication data
A catalogue record for this book is available from the British Library.

© Copyright 1997 by Allen Brown.

First published in 1997 by How To Books Ltd, 3 Newtec Place,
Magdalen Road, Oxford OX4 1RE, United Kingdom.
Tel: (01865) 793806. Fax: (01865) 248780.

Note: The material contained in this book is set out in good faith for general
guidance and no liability can be accepted for loss or expense incurred as a
result of relying in particular circumstances on statements made in the book.
The laws and regulations are complex and liable to change, and readers
should check the current position with the relevant authorities before making
personal arrangements.

Produced for How To Books by Deer Park Productions.
Typeset by Kestrel Data, Exeter.
Printed and bound in Great Britain by Cromwell Press, Broughton Gifford,
Melksham, Wiltshire.

Contents

List of Illustrations

Preface

Over the past few years the number of universities in Britain has increased as a result of polytechnics and some colleges of higher education being reclassified as universities. Consequently there are now considerably more opportunities in all aspects of higher education, including education to Master's degree level. There is every indication that this expansion will continue for the foreseeable future.

This book aims to help the reader who is considering embarking on a part-time or full-time Master's degree programme and the issues covered include:

- The advantages of possessing a Master's degree.

- How to choose a relevant subject and a university.

- Whether to apply for a taught Master's programme or a programme by research only.

- How to decide which is more appropriate – a part-time or full-time programme.

- How to prepare yourself for tackling a Master's degree.

- What to expect from a taught Master's programme.

- How to choose and use the resources required to ensure success.

- How to avoid mistakes and watch out for pitfalls in a higher degree programme.

Whether you are hoping to pursue a taught Master's programme or a programme by research, the **dissertation** or **thesis** is of paramount importance in your assessment and is therefore covered in some detail in Chapter 10. The purpose of the dissertation is to provide you with the opportunity of demonstrating, to the university, what you are capable of doing mainly off your own back. It gives you the opportunity of developing your own ideas and arguments and presenting them as a credible academic exercise.

ACKNOWLEDGEMENT

I should like to express my gratitude to Michael Geary and Martin Roots for patiently reading through the draft of this book and making many useful and helpful suggestions.

Allen Brown
Cambridge 1997

1
Looking at a Master's Degree

In the early 1990s British polytechnics and some colleges of higher education were reclassified as universities. These *new* universities are able to award degrees in their own right. Together with the traditional universities they are offering opportunities for further training beyond that of BSc or BA degrees. With the increase in the number of universities in Britain, access to higher education opportunities has been greatly enhanced. There are over 5,000 Master's degree programmes available in Britain – part-time and full-time.

REASONS FOR WANTING A MASTER'S DEGREE

There are many reasons why you might want to acquire a Master's degree. Having been through the learning process for a first degree or a diploma you may want to keep your academic interest alive. Probably the opportunity did not exist before because of demands on your time or possibly there wasn't a suitable university within easy travelling distance. Whatever the reason, you probably fall into one of the following categories.

Progressing from a first degree
After completing a first taught bachelor's degree you may feel sufficiently interested in your subject to pursue it further. Registering for a Master's degree is an ideal method of continuing your search for knowledge. You may have taken a year out after graduating and feel that you wish to get back into the university system. You may be a graduate who is experiencing difficulty in securing your first job, and registering for a Master's degree is one way of resolving the problem in the short term. Having a higher degree will also enhance your employment propsects – certainly, an added qualification on the CV will not do your prospects any harm.

Finding alternative employment

Alternatively, after working for several years following graduation, you may feel that your current knowledge or experience is so finely tuned in your present job that it may act against you when searching for a future position. Being in possession of a Master's degree would broaden your expertise and make you more marketable. Since the number of graduates is higher today than ever before, the competition for professional positions is correspondingly greater. When applying for a new job you may feel more confident if you have a higher degree to complement your experience.

Staff development

You may find that in the normal course of your employment, your job specification is likely to change. This could come about for several reasons, for example, company downsizing, shifting market strategies or skill redeployment. You may be required to take on new responsibilities and new roles for which you require a form of retraining or staff development. One means of achieving this is to pursue a part-time Master's programme in a subject closely related to your new line of responsibilities. The extra time you will have to allocate to study for the higher degree will certainly demonstrate to your employers that you are taking the retraining seriously.

Improving employment prospects

You may feel that the job opportunities in your present company would be greatly enhanced if you had more qualifications. It is only on very rare occasions that possession of a Master's degree will act against you. It does, after all, command instant respect as you will be recognised as having expert knowledge in your field. It may be in your interest to enquire amongst the senior management whether your company would be prepared to offer you any incentive to do a Master's degree part-time – either financially or through remission.

Enhancing your employer's R&D profile

One of the major reasons why much of British industry persistently fails to develop in the high technology market is neglect of Research and Development (R&D) as compared with our major competitors, Germany, the USA and Japan. This is amply demonstrated by the plethora of high technology imports from these nations into Britain.

Although the lack of R&D skills in Britain remains acute, many companies are attempting to address the deficiency by encouraging some of their graduate employees to register at universities to research for a higher degree part-time. This could be part of a company-wide scheme to encourage skill updating amongst its employees, and will have the effect of elevating the company's R&D profile. You may be in the fortunate position of benefiting from such an incentive. If such a scheme doesn't already exist within your company it may be worthwhile, and of course to your advantage, to pursue the possibility with senior management.

Formalising your interest in a subject

It's quite possible that you've had a lifetime interest in one particular subject. You may spend a lot of time working on the subject without having a clear objective in mind. Having an objective, such as gaining a higher degree, will give you the opportunity of consolidating your knowledge into a well-ordered framework. It can act as a goal and thereby direct your progression in the subject.

MASTER'S DEGREES IN THE UK

Within the British university system there are a variety of Master's degrees on offer within two basic formats:

1. **A taught degree programme** in which the candidate will be assessed by examinations, assignments and presentations and is required to submit a written dissertation.

2. **By research only,** when a candidate will have a research project and will be assessed on the results of their investigation submitted as a thesis. The candidate will have an oral examination to **defend** his/her thesis.

Examples of Master's degrees currently being offered in British universities include:

- MA – Master of Arts
- M.Sc. – Master of Science
- M.Mus. – Master of Music
- LL.M – Master of Laws
- M.Ed. – Master of Education
- M.Eng. – Master of Engineering
- MBA – Master of Business Administration
- M.Phil. – Master of Philosophy
- M.Res. – Master of Research.

In general the first seven of this list relate to taught Master's programmes whereas the M.Phil. is used as a title for a Master's *research* degree (see Chapters 3 and 4). However, there are exceptions to this rule, depending on the institution running the programmes. Incidentally, an M.Phil. degree is by no means reserved for philosophy, but is normally awarded for performing research in any subject.

The majority of taught Master's programmes in humanities will end with an MA award whereas in the sciences the final award is an M.Sc. The exceptions are the M.Mus. for music and LL.M for law. Some universities, especially those that have a strong engineering emphasis, will also have an M.Eng. degree as the final award.

The M.Res. degree is relatively new and aims to prepare candidates, working in industry, to conduct research in their chosen field. Completion of an M.Res. degree will serve as a suitable entry qualification for a Ph.D. programme.

At the end of the day all Master's degrees awarded by British universities carry the same weight. Candidates who fail to complete a Master's programme but have accumulated sufficient credits may be awarded a post-graduate diploma (Pg.Dip.).

CHOOSING A SUBJECT FOR A MASTER'S PROGRAMME

An important question to ask is, *What subject should you do a Master's degree in?* The answer will depend on several factors which need to be considered carefully:

● What is your subject area of interest?

● Do you have the necessary ability and resolve to complete the degree?

● How much will it improve your job prospects?

● If you choose to do it part-time, can you find a course in a university within easy travelling distance?

● Can you find financial support for the degree programme?

If you are already a graduate, the natural choice of subject for a Master's will be an extension of your undergraduate degree.

Although in many instances this may be inappropriate, you should have at least a strong interest in the subject area of your proposed degree programme.

Employment in the 1990s, even for graduates, is difficult and you should really think of a Master's degree as a means of enhancing your employment prospects. Although some employers tend to place more emphasis on experience than on paper qualifications, a Master's degree is still regarded as an excellent means of updating skills.

Choosing a university

Travelling distance may strongly influence your choice of university especially if you are likely to become a part-time student. Information regarding available postgraduate degree courses can be gleaned from the university's postgraduate prospectus. Most of the newer universities also have open days which give an opportunity for prospective postgraduate students to see what's available. Alternatively, ring up the head of department of your subject area and ask what's on offer. You will find that he is usually quite amenable and will probably arrange for you to visit the university. During your visit you will probably have the opportunity of meeting members of the academic staff who specialise in your subject area.

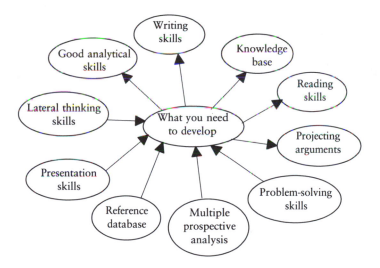

Fig. 1. Overview of the skills required during a Master's degree programme.

ASSESSING YOUR SUITABILITY

To work through a Master's programme and achieve a higher degree will require a lot of personal application. It will make demands on you intellectually, consume a lot of your time and involve sacrifices. By this we mean sacrifices of other pursuits, as you have to be extremely careful not to spread yourself and your personal resources too thinly. If you fall into this trap you will not complete enough work to merit an award of a Master's degree. Some of the skills required for a Master's degree are shown in Figure 1.

Are you qualified?

Before you can register for a Master's degree at a university you will have to satisfy the university that you possess the appropriate qualifications and experience. The following are **general guidelines** as to what may be required:

- *Honours degree*: if you possess a good honours degree (first or second class), there is a very good chance of being accepted.

- *Pass degree, HND or other diploma*: in this case, to be accepted onto a Master's programme will be somewhat more difficult. Your prospects will be improved if you have several years of relevant work experience after graduating.

- *No formal qualifications*: in these circumstances your acceptance onto a higher degree programme will depend on your current employment position and whether you are able to demonstrate that the standard of your working practice is sufficiently high to warrant comparison with a graduate in a similar position. Your case would be strongly helped if you have any publications in your name, preferably in refereed journals. Membership of a recognised institution would also be an advantage. Your prospects will be particularly difficult if you wish to pursue research in a subject which has no relevance to your present employment position. However, if you have a number of publications in well-known specialist journals you stand a better chance of being accepted. If you can also demonstrate that you have been active in a form of continuing education by updating your skills over the last few years, this will be seen in a very favourable light.

University regulations for entry on an M.Phil.
The above entry qualifications are applicable for both taught and research programmes. However, sometimes there are special cases for M.Phil. research programmes. To give you a better understanding of what's required when you are pursuing research for a Master's programme, it may be helpful to quote from the *Research Degrees Regulations for Anglia Polytechnic University*:

An applicant not holding the normal qualification for entry shall be considered on his/her merits and in relation to the nature and scope of the programme of work proposed. In considering an applicant in this category, the Research Degrees Committee shall look for evidence of the candidate's ability and background knowledge in relation to the proposed research. Professional experience, publications, written reports or other appropriate evidence of accomplishment shall be taken into consideration. The Research Degrees Committee may require an applicant to pass an externally assessed qualifying examination at final year honours degree level before registration is approved. An applicant wishing to be considered under this regulation shall include in the application for registration the names of two suitable persons whom the University may consult concerning the candidate's academic attainment and fitness for research.

Whatever qualifications you have, you should make enquiries with the university with which you wish to register. They will have a postgraduate prospectus that will set out their entrance policy for mature students wishing to do research.

OBTAINING MORE INFORMATION

There are a number of sources of information on Master's degrees taught at British universities.

CRAC
Postgrad: Careers Research and Advisory Centre (CRAC) is published annually by Hobsons Press, Cambridge. Although it is quite an expensive publication, you should be able to find a copy in your local public library.

Hobsons also produce a publication entitled *Postgrad: the Students' Guide* (Biblios Publishers Distribution, Tel: (01403) 710851) which is a free publication that lists Master's programmes in the UK. A directory of graduate studies on the Internet can be accessed at the Web site:

```
http://www.hobsons.co.uk
```

The postgraduate prospectus

Every British university publishes each year a postgraduate prospectus which contains information on available taught Master's degree programmes. It will most probably also have information on research opportunities leading to M.Phil. and Ph.D. degrees. Many universities also publish course brochures which give more information than generally found in the postgraduate prospectus. Telephone the universities you are interested in to ask for a copy of their prospectus. (See the telephone numbers in Appendix A.) You may be asked whether you want information on taught Master's degrees or research degrees. It's common practice to include an application form with the prospectus and in general the application forms are different for the two types of degree.

The Higher Educational Careers Service Unit (CSU)

The CSU supports the work of careers services in universities and produces publications which advertise postgraduate vacancies in British universities. *Prospects Postgrad* is used by the majority of universities to advertise Master's and Doctorate programmes. They also produce the publication *Prospects Today* which advertises immediate vacancies for graduates. CSU can be contacted on (0161) 236 9816. Alternatively they can be accessed on the Internet Web site:

```
http://www.prospect.csu.man.ac.uk
```

Newspapers and magazines

The Times newspaper publishes three times a year a list of Master's degree courses running in British universities. In February, it's a single supplement whereas in June and September it's a couple of pages in every edition over a period of a week.

The Times Higher Education Supplement (THES) is also used by British universities to advertise their Master's degree programmes. Normally reference will also be made to possible funding if the courses are full-time. If you are interested in science Master's programmes (especially live science) one useful source of information is the *New Scientist* magazine.

Looking at several universities

If you are thinking of becoming a full-time student and are without any domestic commitments (family and/or house-owner) then you can look round the whole country for the ideal Master's degree for your needs. However, many full-time postgraduates in their twenties have chosen a university within travelling distance of their parental home to reduce their personal expenses. If you're likely to be a part-time student your choices for a university will probably be limited, determined primarily by the travelling distance. If, however, you live in a catchment area within travelling distance of several universities it's a worthwhile exercise to review a number of universities and what they have to offer. By doing this you will be able to gain an overall impression of each university and whether their higher degree courses really coincide with what you want to do.

Funding

If you are intending to pursue a full-time Master's degree, whether a taught degree or by research, you should consider very carefully the funding available. Many full-time Master's degrees are funded by one of the research councils (see Appendix B), which provide a number of bursaries for the duration of the course, usually one year. The bursary is sufficient to pay the university fees and provide living expenses for the student. Although you will find many higher degree programmes in universities, not all are funded. If you are considering a full-time Master's degree programme it's in your interest to find a course that has a bursary attached to it, otherwise you will be expected to pay for everything which may amount to several thousands of pounds. You will have to decide whether it's really worth it in the long run.

CHECKLIST

- Look in your *Yellow Pages* under Education to see which universities are within travelling distance of your home.

- Perform a careful analysis of your spare time to see if you can afford at least fourteen hours a week for the additional study.

- If you are in full-time employment, check with your line manager to ensure there will be no conflict of interest if you choose to do a Master's degree part-time.

● Discuss with your line manager the possibility of your company paying the fees. This may happen if the course you wish to pursue is of interest to your company as it may be considered as skill updating.

CASE STUDIES

Using a Master's degree to gain new skills for your job

Teresa holds a BA in History and has been working in the External Relations Office in her company. A medium-term objective of her company is to heighten its profile by using Multimedia Technology. Teresa has been asked to oversee this task and requires suitable Staff Development.

Since Teresa's degree is in History she will require more than just a skill update to fulfil her remit. She needs to ascertain from her line manager:

● the level of investment for the multimedia facility
● the nature and extent of the multimedia operation
● future expansion of the facility.

If her company is serious about its expansion plans, Teresa will need to acquire new Information Technology skills. However, since it's a medium-term objective, Teresa could look for a part-time post-graduate M.Sc. course on Multimedia Technology, preferably at a university within easy travelling distance of her home. By reading through the course brochure and contacting the admissions tutor, Teresa should be able to determine whether the material covered on the course is relevant to her future needs.

Gaining an LL.M to help secure a lectureship

Dennis is a law graduate and has been working as a solicitor for four years. He is thinking about becoming a part-time law lecturer.

It's commonplace for solicitors to be employed part-time by universities to give lecture modules. There is usually a significant difference in salaries between a practising solicitor and a lecturer, and Dennis is therefore advised to retain his position in his legal company. He should, however, consider doing a Master of Law (LL.M) degree part-time at a university within easy travelling distance of his home and practice. Dennis will need to:

- contact the admissions tutor in the law department, to obtain information on the LL.M degree and what opportunities there are for lecturing part-time

- determine whether his employer will pay for his university fees

- determine the remission time he can have to pursue the Master's programme.

Progressing onto a Master's degree after graduating

Ken has just graduated in Environmental Science and has gained an Upper Second in his B.Sc. honours classification. He wants to continue with his studies by doing a full-time M.Sc. in Environmental Toxicology.

Since Ken does not have any family, he is free to move to any part of the country that has a university running M.Sc. courses in his subject. This is quite fortunate since there are relatively few universities offering such options. To find out which universities do, he could consult *CRAC* (see above). On finding a suitable institution, Ken should contact the admissions tutor, by telephone, letter or email, and determine if there is funding available from any of the research councils (see Appendix B).

DISCUSSION POINTS

1. Will a Master's degree improve your job prospects?
2. How much time do you have available for doing a Master's degree?
3. How determined are you to see it through to a satisfactory conclusion?
4. How supportive are your family likely to be?
5. What level of support are you likely to receive from your employer?

2
Looking at a Taught Master's Degree

A taught Master's programme usually comprises lectures, seminars, presentations and laboratory practice (if appropriate). The common assessment methods include examinations, assignments and the writing of a dissertation. Most full-time Master's degree programmes last for one academic year whereas the part-time programmes last for two years.

REVIEWING FULL-TIME AND PART-TIME COURSES

The majority of British universities offer Master's degree programmes on either a full-time or part-time basis. Potential candidates who are currently in full-time employment will probably be attracted to part-time Master's programmes, whereas if you are a fresh graduate your interest will be in a full-time Master's degree. Although all universities run Master's programmes they are not always run in both full-time and part-time modes – check with the university you are interested in. In general, part-time courses take twice as long as the full- time equivalent but cost less. Full-time fees are considerably more than part-time fees.

ARE YOU QUALIFIED FOR A TAUGHT MASTER'S COURSE?

The entry qualifications for a taught Master's degree are not too dissimilar to those outlined in Chapter 1 for an M.Phil. degree. You will normally be expected to have a first degree or equivalent in a suitably related subject to that of the intended Master's programme. Depending on the competition for places on the course, you may be asked for a second class honours degree at least. But sometimes this condition may be relaxed provided you are able to show competence in the subject area of the degree. This should be gained either from your work experience or from articles or papers you have had published in a related field.

22

GETTING FINANCIAL SUPPORT

If you are hoping to pursue a Master's programme as a full-time postgraduate student you are well advised to seek a course that has studentships attached to it. A limited number of studentships are given to some universities by funding councils to run Master's programmes. These are normally only applicable to full-time Master's degrees. If you are a fresh graduate it's highly likely that you're carrying a Student Loan debt. The 'good news' is that a Master's studentship or bursary has provision for the university fees and your living expenses, but little else, so you will not be required to start paying off your loan from your bursary.

If you can't secure a place on a Master's programme with funding, look for another university or another course that does have funding. If you choose to pay for it yourself you may very well end up with a debt of several thousand pounds.

If you have a good first degree and a Master's degree (or even a Ph.D.) in a very sought after subject (such as electronics) you may be tempted to enter the **brain drain.** You would then leg-it to the USA and forget about the debt (until you want to return, that is). This, however, is not a mode of conduct that you should subscribe to.

Funding councils

In the UK there are several funding councils that provide a limited number of studentships (bursaries) to universities to support postgraduate students on Master's programmes. Normally to qualify for a studentship you need at least a Second Class Honours degree. Some funding councils are now stipulating an Upper Second or First to qualify. Check with the admissions tutor on the conditions. (See Appendix B for a list of institutions in the UK that sponsor postgraduate research.)

Generally when you see a Master's degree programme advertised in *The Guardian* or in *New Scientist* it will state whether bursaries are available and what is required to secure one. Generally these are only available for full-time programmes. Some local education authorities support Master's programmes but these are quite rare. You may get funding as part of a retraining scheme operated by a local employment agency. This is especially true for part-time programmes. Ask at your Citizens' Advice Bureau whether they have any information on course funding in higher education.

FILLING IN THE APPLICATION FORM

This is an important step in your application for a place on a Master's programme as it indicates to the admissions tutor several things about your character. There was a time when you could fill it in on a typewriter but since these are rare these days you may have to rely on your best handwriting. In fact it's your first examination on the Master's programme and it's advisable to draft out the answers to each section on a photocopy of the original before filling in the form proper. This way you will know exactly what to say and minimise any mistakes. If there's a lot of competition for places on the course your answers and presentation on the application form may very well influence the admissions tutor. He/she may reject you even without an interview. Take time to consider your answers carefully.

Referees

You will also be expected to supply the names of at least one referee who can vouch for your academic credentials. If you've come straight from another university your previous tutor is a normal choice. However, if you have been out of higher education for several years try and find someone within your company who is familiar with your skills and work performance.

Your interview

The second hurdle in achieving a place on a Master's programme is the interview at the university normally with the admissions tutor. The nature of these interviews can vary greatly. If the tutor has any doubt regarding your suitability it's possible that you may be expected to answer several technical questions which can be an unpleasant experience even if you know the answers. However, in general this is not a common practice.

It is more likely that the admissions tutor will want to know why you want to come onto the course and gauge the level of interest and enthusiasm you have for the subject. Do not attempt to be clever during the interview. Chances are that the admissions tutor has been researching the subject for years and knows vastly more about it than you.

What you should get from the interview

When it comes to your turn to ask questions by all means ask about the facilities the university has to support the Master's programme. Also ask about:

- the teaching routines and the delivery modes
- the number of students in the class
- access to tutors outside the lecture periods
- support materials and resources.

Asking searching questions has the explicit benefit of establishing a rapport between you and the admissions tutor. You may also meet other lecturers and it's important for you to feel comfortable with what's on offer. If you are applying for a full-time course you should confirm your position with regard to an available studentship to support you throughout the year.

BEING A POSTGRADUATE STUDENT

If your application had been successful you will be offered a place on the Master's programme. Your first week even if you are a part-time student will involve some sort of induction – this basically introduces you to the resources within the university (the library and the computer centre). The normal mode of teaching is the lecture. There are a variety of lecturing techniques including **chalk and talk** (see Figure 2), **overheads and talk** or just **talk**.

Fig. 2. Chalk and talk is still an effective teaching method.

These days 'overheads and talk' is more popular especially for higher degree courses. The lecturer has a mass of transparencies for the overhead projector and also supplies you with a booklet containing copies of each one. There is an inherent danger with this teaching method. The transparency will only contain a skeletal framework of each topic and most of the information will be imparted verbally. You will be expected to make notes from what's been said to you. If you think that you are missing much of the material, you can ask the lecturer if you can record the lecture using a Micro Cassette Dictating Machine. Do not use one of these unless you have the permission of the lecturer – it is a matter of courtesy to ask. Once you get home in the evening review your lecture notes and fill in the gaps. Don't leave it – do it while the information is fresh in your memory.

What I Don't Understand Book (WIDUB)

As you read through your lecture notes you will come across material the significance of which you failed to grasp or understand during the lecture. In many subjects, even at undergraduate level, it's important to have an exercise book (a **WIDUB** or What I Don't Understand Book) where you enter questions from your lecture notes relating to material you don't understand. After all, it's not the material that you do understand that causes problems, it's what you don't understand. Once you've made entries in your WIDUB, go and see the lecturer and ask him/her to explain the point of confusion. Once you understand you can draw a red line through the question in your WIDUB.

Practical work

Many Master's degree programmes have a practical element as part of the teaching schedule. You must get yourself a logbook (or a lab-book) and record what you do in your practical sessions. You may have sessions of using software on PC. As you are learning your way around the software, make notes of what you are learning. This, after all, is part of the knowledge that you are seeking by coming on the course. If it has value you should record it so that you can refer to it at a later date. Don't rely on your memory. On some programmes part of the assessment scheme is the write-up in the logbook – you cannot afford to neglect it. If it's new, log it – and don't forget to date every entry.

Tutorials and exercises

The well-known phrase 'practice makes proficiency' is as applicable to Master's programmes as any other walk of life. Once you have gained knowledge you need to use it to develop skills and the most effective way of achieving this is through exercises. In a university environment exercises are usually discussed in a tutorial setting. You will be allocated a supervisor or tutor, part of whose job description is to monitor your progress and provide advice and guidance. This may involve the setting of tutorial exercises, especially if you are on a science or engineering programme. It is very important that you spend time working through these exercises as this enhances your understanding of the subject.

THINKING ABOUT ASSESSMENT METHODS

Within a Master's degree programme there will be several assessment methods each carrying a proportion of weight depending on its individual significance. These could include:

- examinations
- assignments
- tutorial exercises
- laboratory work
- presentations and seminars
- oral examination
- dissertation.

Some Master's degree programmes dispense with examinations completely and the principal assessment method is the written assignment, but it must be stressed that this is not common practice.

Examinations

Examinations have never been popular with students, but in general they are a fact of university life. They are one of the main assessment methods and a lot of emphasis is placed on them. Examination questions are usually constructed in such a way as to test the student's understanding of the subject and whether they can apply their knowledge to solve a problem. However, it must be said of many programmes that a pass can be obtained without the student having any idea of how to successfully apply their newly gained knowledge. Since you are on a Master's programme, it is assumed that you have gained sufficient maturity not to leave the revision to the last couple of weeks before the examination. Anyway, for a Master's degree it should be more a case of refreshing than revising.

Examination strategy
When sitting a written examination the golden rule is:

Read the questions very carefully.

Although this is an obvious thing to do, it's always a source of amazement for lecturers to find students who don't actually do this. Only answer what is asked. Very often students make the tragic mistake of writing everything they know on the question's subject matter. This is a total waste of time and effort which a student can little afford.

Success with a written examination is an exponential process. The first 40 per cent of the marks can be obtained with relatively little effort, while the remaining 60 per cent are disproportionately more difficult to reach. Reaching the last 10 per cent (gaining 90 per cent +) is only achieved by exceptional students. An examination strategy should include the following:

● Read the questions carefully. You are usually given 10 minutes reading time before the examination begins.

● Spend an equal amount of time on each question. Divide your allotted time by the number of questions you are asked to attempt.

● Plan your answers, and if it's a multiple-part question make sure you answer every part and label it clearly.

● If you are an average student, concentrate on reaching the first 50 – 60 per cent of the marks on each question.

● Only answer the required number of questions. Answering more indicates poor time management. You would do better concentrating on the questions you have attempted. Examiners become very annoyed at seeing excess questions to mark and the last thing you want is the examiner to be in a bad frame of mind.

● Don't panic. If you do, just jot down the points you remember – the rest will follow in good time.

● If you find you are running out of time, list your answer using bullet points.

Improving your handwriting
Before you sit any examinations it may be worthwhile reviewing the quality of your handwriting. If you produce illegible scroll you may lose marks because the examiner may miss points in your argument. Legible handwriting is only a matter of practice. Get yourself a fountain pen; owing to the high surface friction on the paper you will be able to exercise greater control over it and your writing. If you've had problems with examinations in the past, it would be worth your while to read *How To Pass Exams Without Anxiety* by David Acres (How To Books 1995). He gives a great deal of good advice that students would do well to heed when preparing for and sitting examinations.

Assignments

Mid-term (or semester) assignments are commonplace on Master's programmes and you are usually given several weeks to complete a given assignment. The hand-in date is crucial – it is common practice to penalise a student if they hand in assignments late. Assignments usually have several sections and there is usually no unique solution to the problem(s) set. The purpose of the assignment is to determine:

● how well you understand the aim of the assignment
● your methodology (how you tackle the assignment)
● the rationale of your approach
● the soundness of your answer or solution.

Unlike examinations, if there is an aspect of the assignment that is unclear you should be able to discuss it with the lecturer that assigned it. However, you should be careful in how you express your difficulties. Stating outright that you don't understand the question indicates that you have made little effort in reading the assignment and raises doubts about whether you should be on the Master's programme in the first place. The lecturer will expect you to have had a stab at it beforehand. You should do this anyway, then ask whether you are on the right track. At least this way you will have indicated that you have thought about it before rushing headlong into his/her office. It's worth remembering that the work you are set is at Master's degree level and you should know what is required. If, initially, you are uncertain what is expected from you at this level – ask!

Assignment strategy
As with examinations, there is a strategy that you can adopt in tackling assignments:

● Make a start as soon as possible. Whatever you do, don't leave it to the week before the hand-in date. You can never do justice to an assignment by allocating such a limited amount of time to it.

● You will realise, once you make a start, that there is more to it than you originally thought from your first reading. If you are late in starting you will not have time to develop the full aspects of the assignment.

● Plan your assignment and get it clear in your mind what is required. If there are doubts, discuss them with the lecturer or even your supervisor in the manner prescribed above. During the discussion he/she will ascertain your understanding of the assignment and attempt to make you think about it – part of the learning process.

● Don't forget to include at the end of the assignment a bibliography of the works you have referenced during its preparation.

● If you have to use laboratory resources or computers for the assignment, remember that in the last week there will be pressure on them from other students on the course working on the assignment.

● If possible complete and hand in the assignment a week before it is due. This has the psychological effect of not having to compete with your peers to finish the assignment – a real source of stress.

● Do not miss lectures in order to finish assignments. This indicates poor time management and is considered inappropriate practice for Master's degree students.

● If you know in advance that an assignment will be late, notify the tutor as early as possible. It is appreciated that we all have lives outside the university and that external pressures can often disrupt the best plans.

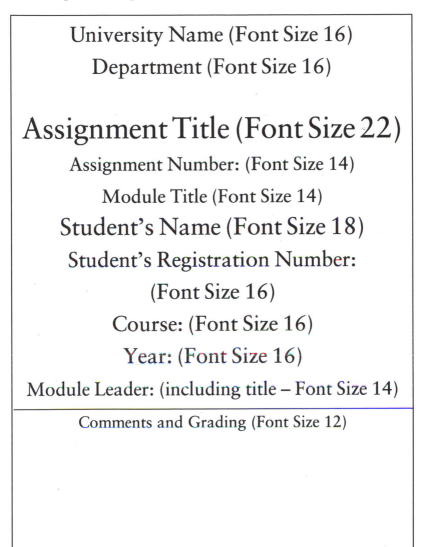

University Name (Font Size 16)

Department (Font Size 16)

Assignment Title (Font Size 22)

Assignment Number: (Font Size 14)

Module Title (Font Size 14)

Student's Name (Font Size 18)

Student's Registration Number:

(Font Size 16)

Course: (Font Size 16)

Year: (Font Size 16)

Module Leader: (including title – Font Size 14)

Comments and Grading (Font Size 12)

Fig. 3. Typical layout of the front page of an assignment.

- If you do hand in an assignment late, you had better have a rock solid reason, not a pitiful excuse. It's a matter of common courtesy to discuss the issue of the delay with the lecturer involved.

Wordprocessing
You will need to acquire wordprocessing skills for producing your assignment on A4-size paper. Handwritten versions are no longer acceptable since computer facilities are provided for all students. If you can't use a wordprocessor, find out how to. Figure 3 is an example of a covering page for an assignment. As you can see, the bottom third of the page is left blank for the examiner's comments. Some very useful information on assignment writing is given in *Writing an Assignment* by Pauline Smith (How To Books, 3rd edition 1997).

Presentations
In addition to assignments, a number of institutions also use presentations as a means of assessment. It is likely that you will be expected to give a presentation on research for your dissertation project. Presentations are important and serve as a valuable form of communication. If you expect to hold down a high profile job, in whatever walk of life, your presentation skills will be frequently called upon.

It is common practice to have project presentations over one or possibly two days depending on the number of students on the course. For the presentation you will be assigned between twenty and thirty minutes. During this time you are expected to discuss the significance of your dissertation project. The presentation should fall into four sections:

1. Introduction
2. Methodology and design
3. Results
4. Conclusion.

Creating a good impression
During the presentation you will be expected to present yourself and your project goals in the best possible light. Even if you have not achieved the expected objectives you should nevertheless present the work as a positive accomplishment. You should make an effort to dress for the occasion in order to create a good starting impression. The main tools you will use in your presentation will be the overhead projector, for your transparencies, and a pointer (either telescopic or laser). Here are a number of points that you should heed:

- At the start of the presentation explain who you are and what the title of your presentation is.

- Use cue cards as a prompt for the items you wish to discuss and the order in which you wish to introduce them.

- When producing overhead transparencies do not put too much information on each one.

- To produce overheads you should use a PC linked to a colour inkjet printer. Colour is one important feature for imparting information. Large fonts are a must – all text must be readable from the back of the room. If possible, try it out beforehand.

- Handwritten overheads create a poor impression. They indicate that you not taking the presentation seriously and you are failing to sell yourself.

- When discussing material on an overhead, use your pointer on the screen *not* on the overhead projector itself. The latter is very unprofessional and on numerous occasions I have seen students standing between the projector and the screen completely oblivious to the fact that only their shadow is visible on the screen. Embarrassment follows when it's pointed out what they are doing, resulting in them losing their way.

- Each transparency should be on the projector for at least 20 seconds. Only having a quick glimpse of a transparency is very annoying.

- Do not read large chunks of text from your notes. It is *your* project in which you have invested a great deal of time. You should therefore be sufficiently familiar with the material not to have to resort to excessive use of notes.

- Speak slowly. Do not rush the presentation otherwise the significant points of your talk will not get over to your audience, and again you will be seen as unprofessional. It's highly likely that during your employment you will be expected sometimes to give presentations. It is not only you on show but your company as well – you can't afford to screw it up.

● Nerves can be a problem especially if you have not given a presentation before. They can be controlled provided you do not rush. Think about what you are going to say. If your mind goes blank, refer to your cue cards.

● Before you give the presentation do a rehearsal and time yourself making sure that you do not exceed the allotted time. Twenty minutes may seem a long time but it passes very quickly when you have a lot to say.

Feedback
A characteristic of presentations that you may not be aware of, especially if you've not given one before, is the absence of feedback. Normal conversations between two or more people are interactive. During a presentation there is no feedback or stimulus to respond to and many people find this very disconcerting – be prepared for it. At the end of the presentation a few minutes will be allocated to questions. Normally this is the easiest part because you start getting feedback and stimulus from your audience which you can respond to positively.

Seminars

You can think of a seminar as a mini presentation where you are expected to discuss or review a particular topic given to you by your tutor or supervisor. Unlike a formal presentation a seminar has a higher degree of interactive discussion from the listeners. It is quite acceptable for you to read your material from written text but you should do this in such a way that it flows freely and has a high degree of continuity. Your seminar material should contain from 500 to 1,500 words. By all means use slides or overheads to support your argument if you need them.

A major part of the seminar is the discussion that follows the presentation of your material. When appraising your performance your tutor (or lecturer) will be looking for:

● soundness of argument
● the depth of your research
● your understanding of the topic
● how effectively you use references to support your argument.

You will also be assessed on how well you respond to the discussion that follows and how well you handle yourself when challenged – how effective you are at defending your argument.

Laboratory work

If you follow a Master's programme that involves lab work you will probably be assessed on it. Working on PCs may also be regarded as lab work. Whichever the case, you will be provided with a set of lab exercises which you are expected to perform. It is essential that you have a lab-book for writing up your exercises. It is good practice to have a logbook where you enter all the results and any other observations that you make during the course of the exercises. Once complete you then write it up in the lab-book which will be marked. Each exercise should take a similar format:

1. Title and date.
2. Brief description of exercise.
3. Brief description of method.
4. Results in either tabular or graphical form.
5. Discussion of results and other observations made during the exercise.

It's commonplace these days for graphs to be generated, using a suitable PC software package, and inserted into the logbook. Make sure with the tutor overseeing the lab session that this is acceptable practice before you do it.

Vivas or oral exams

During the period of your Master's programme you will invariably be asked to undergo a number of vivas or oral exams normally relating to the progress of your dissertation project. The format comprises two or more lecturers and one student – you. Vivas can be rather stressful for the student especially if their performance has not been as good as expected. The purpose of the viva is to:

● Formally monitor the progress (or lack of progress) of the project.

● Offer advice, guidance and constructive criticism on the direction of your project.

● Assess how well you have achieved a set of objectives, of which you will have been given prior notice.

● Discuss what measures need to be adopted to ensure that

sufficient material has been produced to secure success in the project.

If your performance has been dismal don't be surprised if you have a hard time. This can have quite a sobering effect by stimulating you into action. Remember it will be done for your own good.

DISSERTATION PROJECT

The final requirement for a taught Master's will be to choose a project, carry out research into your selected topic, and write up a dissertation (a report of your research studies and your analysis and/or findings). This is covered in detail in Chapter 10.

CHECKLIST

● Explore the possibilities of financial support.

● Fill in the application form carefully and prepare for your interview.

● Make sure that you understand the assessment methods for each module on your course.

● During your induction you should be given a course booklet which contains a variety of details on resources, student information and general university procedures. Read through it as soon as you can after registering. Don't neglect it, it's written for your benefit.

CASE STUDIES

Computer resources for an Econometrics Master's
Anni has registered on an MA programme in Econometrics and is wondering about the computer resources she's likely to need for the course.

Like all other higher degree students, Anni will invariably need access to a PC, or better still, should acquire one herself. Anni's subject, econometrics, requires a fair amount of computational analysis and the PC she will need must be up to the job. She will also need statistical software such as **Statgraphics** or **Unistat**. Anni's PC should have a minimum configuration of:

- Pentium P120
- 1-Gbyte hard-disc drive
- 16-Mbyte RAM
- 14-inch colour monitor
- Six-speed CD-ROM drive
- 600-dot/inch laser printer.

Anni should also be able to find the statistical software she needs with an attractive student discount. She should check with the university's computer centre to see what deals are available.

Using a Master's degree to help secure a career change

Sarah, a biology graduate, is an assistant manager in a high street bank, but she has a passion for Marine Biology. She lives close to the sea and is active in local environmental groups. Some day she hopes to change her career to something which involves Marine Biology.

Sarah knows that jobs in Marine Biology are very difficult to come by and if she wants to stand any chance at all of finding a suitable position she must have a proven track record of being actively involved in the subject. One way of achieving this is to secure a Master's degree in a closely related aspect of biology. For Sarah the gamble of giving up her job in the bank to take a full-time Master's degree is too risky, not knowing whether she would get a suitable job in Marine Biology at the end of the course. She should therefore apply for a part-time Master's degree at a university within convenient travelling distance. If she cannot find the higher degree programme that exactly fits her needs but is in a closely related field, she should:

- Contact the admissions tutor at the university and discuss the course with him/her in order to ascertain how much Marine Biology is covered in it.

- Discuss the possibility of doing a dissertation project on an aspect of Marine Biology thereby shifting the emphasis into her subject area of interest.

Using an M.Sc. to gain expertise in PC networking

Clifford has an HND in Computer Science and has been a computer programmer for the last four years. He is a member of the British Computer Society and is aware of the opportunities for people with an expertise in computer networking. Clifford is thinking of taking a suitable Master's degree.

Clifford has the necessary entry qualifications and experience to be accepted onto a taught Master's degree programme. He will have to decide whether he should take a full-time or part-time Master's degree. A full-time degree with a bursary would mean a considerable reduction in his income and if he has a family this may prove to be too much of a sacrifice to make. He has to trade it off against the expectation of securing a better paid job at the end of the one-year course. His alternative is to register on a part-time programme that will take two years, but he can remain employed during this period. His standard of living should therefore not suffer. Having decided between a full-time or part-time course, Clifford's next course of action will involve:

● contacting suitable universities and requesting a copy of their postgraduate prospectus

● finding a suitable course – although it may not be directly related to computer networking, a substantial part of the course may actually be on the subject

● thinking of a suitable subject for his dissertation that would shift the emphasis onto computer networking.

DISCUSSION POINTS

1. What will you have to sacrifice to do a part-time course? Can you afford to do it? Will you really have the time?
2. Are you a good starter but a poor finisher? Have you really got what it takes to complete a Master's programme?
3. Do you need to acquire or develop any skills in relation to the various assessment methods; for example, wordprocessing, making presentations, leading seminar discussions?
4. Have you begun to think about the question or topic you would like to explore in your dissertation?

3
Thinking about a Research Master's Degree

An alternative to a taught Master's degree is a Master's programme consisting of research only. On completion of the research you will submit a thesis of your findings that will be subject to oral examination ('defending your thesis'). If you are thinking about pursuing a Master's research degree your area of research should have an academic basis and must be worthy of investigation. Whether a subject is suitable is one of the questions you need to discuss with lecturers in the department in which you intend to conduct the proposed research.

WHAT'S REQUIRED FOR M.PHIL. RESEARCH

Your choice of subject for pursuing research towards an M.Phil. will probably be determined by your own range of interests. Conducting research in an area that you have no previous knowledge of is not recommended. It is also unlikely that you will be accepted at a university if you fail to demonstrate sufficient prior knowledge of your intended research topic.

When you register at a university for a research degree you will normally be accepted for an M.Phil., although some universities also award M.Sc., M.Eng. and MA degrees as research degrees.

To succeed with your M.Phil. programme you must have sufficient interest to carry you through to a satisfactory completion.

Postgraduate entry

If you already possess a bachelor's degree then it is likely that your area of research will be in a field *related* to your first degree. This rule is usually interpreted in quite a liberal fashion. For instance, if you have a first degree in biology and you want to do research into medical instrumentation, then it is highly unlikely that your first degree gave you a sufficient knowledge of electronics. This would not be an obstacle to your acceptance as it would be assumed that you have already remedied or are prepared to remedy this deficiency through your own industry.

You may well be expected to attend a number of undergraduate lectures to fill in the gaps in your knowledge. This may present a problem for a part-time research student living some distance from the university who may find it difficult to attend lectures during the day.

Embarking on an M.Phil. research programme is a learning process and you must be prepared to be flexible in your outlook.

Non-graduate entry

As stated in Chapter 1, if you do not possess any formal qualifications then your choice of research will probably be restricted to the areas where you are able to demonstrate a sufficient knowledge through your employment record. For example, if you have become a senior manager and have a particular expertise in managerial techniques relating to the automotive industry, it's highly unlikely that you will be accepted to do research into Late Baroque French Harpsichord Music. You are more likely to be considered if you want to research the effects of changing working practices on productivity. If, however, in your spare time, you've published a number of articles on Late Baroque Practices in early music journals, your proposal may very well be considered.

You've got to be realistic in your choice of subject, remembering that it's most likely to be related to your current employment. If this is not the case you will have to provide some strong evidence to support your proposal. These are matters you must sort out during your visit to the university.

Company skill updating programmes

Some companies actively encourage a number of their employees to go on skill updating and retraining programmes. If you are employed in a company which has a progressive attitude to education you might be successful in persuading your Training Director that researching for a higher degree can be regarded as skill updating. You would therefore be eligible to receive the appropriate funding. Should this be the case, you will be afforded the necessary time off work to pursue your research.

A Master's degree and your current employment

If you are in full-time employment and are thinking of registering for a research degree, you would be advised to consider a research topic which is of some relevance to your current employment. After reading through the typical entry qualifications you will recognise which category you fall into. If you fall into the last category of not possessing any formal qualifications at all, you will require every ounce of help to support your case. If you have several years experience working in an industrial or commercial environment with a proven track record of achievement, you can use this in support of your application. Alternatively, if you have amassed a portfolio of publications on a particular subject, your chances of being accepted are considerably enhanced. You will find that many universities have an open policy towards entry qualifications. However, you must be able to demonstrate a track record of achievement that can be classified as academic. Fortunately this is interpreted quite broadly by many universities, especially for professionals who have relevant experience.

What's involved?

As an indication of the requirements for a research degree, here is an extract from the Council of National Academic Awards (CNAA) regulations. Although the CNAA is now defunct, the information is still valid:

Scope: Programmes of research may be proposed in any field of study subject to the requirements that the proposed programme is capable of leading to scholarly research and to its presentation for assessment by appropriate examiners. The written thesis may be supplemented by material in other than written form. All proposed research programmes will be considered for research degree registration on their academic merits and without reference to the concerns or interests of any associated funding body.

M.Phil. Award: The M.Phil. is awarded to a candidate, who having critically investigated and evaluated an approved topic and demonstrated an understanding of research methods appropriate to the chosen field, has presented and defended a thesis, by oral examination, to the satisfaction of the examiners.

Progressing on to a Ph.D. from an M.Phil.

Very often it is the case that when a candidate makes sufficient progress in his/her research on the M.Phil. programme, an opportunity will be provided to transfer registration onto a Doctor of Philosophy (Ph.D.) programme. This is usually at the end of the M.Phil. programme, and the candidate will be expected to perform further research and make an original contribution to knowledge to merit the award of Ph.D.

Ph.D. degrees in the UK
The nature of the doctorate programme in the UK is quite different from that in the USA. A Ph.D. in the USA will take on average five years and may include written examinations. In UK universities, the general consensus is that a candidate has already demonstrated sufficient ability to pass written exams in their first degree or in their taught Master's degree (M.Sc. or MA). In the UK, an M.Phil. and a Ph.D. is by research only and the candidate is given an oral examination after submission of a thesis. There could be exceptions to this general rule – it is not improbable to be asked to sit a number of undergraduate final year exam papers.

Difference between M.Phil. and Ph.D.
The distinction between the two degrees lies in the **original contribution to knowledge** which is expected before the Ph.D. is awarded. When on a Ph.D. programme, you must be particularly aware of the importance of this aspect of your work and you should be directing your efforts to achieving **original knowledge**. (See *How to Get a PhD*, listed under Further Reading at the end of this book.)

PERSONAL QUALITIES FOR RESEARCH

There are a number of issues to consider before you embark on a research programme leading to a higher degree. After all, it is likely to take you a few years to reach your intended goal – the award of the M.Phil. Figure 4 shows an overview of some of the qualities needed to succeed at an M.Phil.

Do you have sufficient motivation?
A difficult question to answer because the nature of your research may be somewhat unpredictable. At the start you will have great enthusiasm and this will provide sufficient impetus for you to get things organised in the early stage of the research – working to schedules and arranging **quality thinking time**. The most remarkable difference between humanity and the other life forms that inhabit this planet is our ability to think, yet it is the most under-used skill we possess: thinking things through in the quietness of one's own mind without external distractions.

Much of your time will be spent in constructive thinking, which

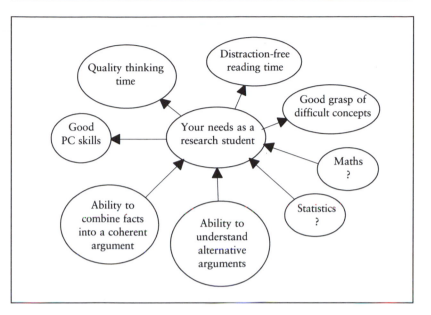

Fig. 4. Overview of requirements of a student on an M.Phil.
research programme.

incidentally is a very lonely occupation. It is highly probable that your early enthusiasm will be replaced by a more dedicated application of your time and resources. If you cannot sustain the required application you will probably lapse. You really have to stick at it and keep to your work schedule if you are going to see it through. Try to avoid taking on other commitments which are likely to impinge on your research time.

What changes are necessary?

Firstly you will have to find the time for your research. However, if you are truly motivated this will not be too difficult. If you currently have many other interests then you will have to sacrifice some of them. Researching for a higher degree is not something that you can perform in parallel with time-consuming pastimes – it requires dedicated application.

One of the simplest ways of finding extra time is to watch less television or even better get rid of it completely, although this may be difficult with other members of the family to consider. You will soon discover that there is no loss being without a television.

Other changes you will have to make involve your attitude and level of open-mindedness you possess. You will have to be prepared to explore new methods of discussing problems using objective reasoning which can be tested.

Need for an open mind

If you are already a professional and very familiar with the knowledge in the area in which you wish to pursue research, you may encounter certain conflicts. It is quite possible that your acquired knowledge has impressed a rigid pattern of thinking on your problem-solving process. Research is about investigating problems, asking questions and exploring alternative perspectives even if seemingly satisfactory solutions currently exist.

Using your acquired knowledge

Your acquired knowledge, gained mainly through experience, will probably have convinced you that your method of solving a problem is the best way. Research is about not just solving problems but investigating problems with an open mind and achieving alternative solutions. You very often hear the American slogan 'if it ain't broke, don't fix it'. Although commendable for the vast majority of applications, a different attitude is appropriate for the researcher, who will always question conventional wisdom. Sometimes this results in innovative alternatives which offer advantages and advancements in knowledge.

Having the right attitude

You must be careful of attitudes like, 'I have always tackled it this way, it achieves results, why should I change?' If you do not have an open mind you are likely to encounter problems with your supervisor because they may not possess your experience to the same degree, but they will possess a greater and broader understanding of your subject in general. You may resent their questioning of what you think you know best. As a new researcher you must try and rid yourself of preconceived, single-track approaches – you will need to apply lateral thinking to your thought processes (see Edward DeBono's book, listed under Further Reading). This will bring more open-mindedness to your powers of reasoning during your quest for further understanding.

Thinking for yourself

Although in the early stages of your research your supervisor will be presenting ideas and suggestions to you, at some stage you will be expected to generate your own. After all, your supervisor will be trying to teach you to think about problems in the same way that he/she does. Your own ideas will only come from your own constructive thinking.

Research needs **quality thinking time** where you will quietly sit and consider possible solutions to issues that your research has thrown up. Having reached what appears to be an answer, do not be tempted to stop there. There may be a better answer lying further on, which you would probably reach if you continued thinking about the problem. You have to find time for thinking through your research problems.

Pitching your project at the right level
There may be a gap between your intellectual capacity and your desire to achieve something significant. There are two extremes that you should be aware of:

- On the one hand, there is no point in choosing a Micky Mouse project which makes no demands on you intellectually. You will run the risk of not reaching the required standard which will probably result in, at best, a lengthy rework or at worst a fail.

- On the other hand, if you choose a project which is well beyond your personal ability to investigate adequately, you will run the risk of not achieving anything at all. Your time will be spent floundering over problems whose analysis is beyond your grasp.

You must therefore try to assess your own intellectual strengths and limitations and choose a research project which will **stretch your abilities** but not exceed them. By doing this you will achieve the effect of exercising your intellect and gain something of significance in your research.

Do you have enough maths?
It is quite possible that the research programme that you embark on will require a proficiency in the application of some mathematical techniques; for example, finding trends or patterns or behaviour, or performing statistical analysis. Using mathematics and understanding its significance is a skill which is acquired by practice. Although some people are born with a natural appitude for maths, others have to develop it like any other skill.

Using a personal computer to do maths
The good news is that this is where the personal computer comes into its own. The PC is extremely effective at performing maths operations, however complex. Whether you need to brush up on your maths knowledge or acquire new skills will depend largely on the nature of your research. The types of software packages you should be looking at include:

- Mathcad (see page 114)
- Matlab
- Maple V.

All these run on a PC and it's highly likely that your university will have some if not all of these packages available for your use. They offer a high degree of visualisation and excellent tools for investigating. Not only can you have 3D graphics but also animations to show the dynamics of a model.

Don't forget about statistics
If your research is of an empirical testing nature you will invariably require some knowledge of applied statistics. Your university supervisors will be able to advise you of this. There is a good chance that you will be able to attend some of the undergraduate lectures on statistics given in the university if you so require. Again the bulk of statistical processing can be performed on a PC and your university will have a number of statistical software packages for you to use. These will probably include:

- StatGraphics
- SSPS
- S-Plus.

These packages tend to be quite expensive and normally you will use the university's computers to access them. There are also a number of (much cheaper) **shareware** programs that perform statistical operations, but check first as far as you can that they will meet your needs.

HOW LONG WILL IT TAKE?

This will depend on several factors. Some very able students (the lucky ones) have achieved an M.Phil. in eighteen months, but this is the exception and not the norm. It depends on how well your research is directed, not only by your supervisor but also by your own commonsense. All research students know that the shortest path between two points is a straight line, but this is not necessarily the route they take.

Typical programme duration

The now defunct CNAA had the following set of times which can act as a useful guide:

- Full-time, 18 months minimum, 36 months maximum.
- Part-time, 30 months minimum, 48 months maximum.

All universities will have their own minimum and maximum periods; however, they are not likely to be too dissimilar to the above times. A question often asked by the new research student relates to the minimum time. A question asked by the veteran research student is whether they can have another year. You need to find your own rhythm and speed and work accordingly.

Dangers

You will find that the above periods are really quite generous, but you do risk two main dangers if you are running late:

- Firstly, you may lose the commitment to keep going and to see it through.

- Secondly, the cost of keeping your registration up with the university may deter you.

It is, however, the former problem that causes the most difficulties. If the work is extended over too long a period the interest can wane.

The good news

Having discussed several aspects that the new research student should be aware of, it is fair to point out that performing research can be immensely rewarding. Acquiring the techniques of analysis and discussing the relevance of your findings with your supervisors and possibly with other research students is very satisfying. The challenge of tackling an issue that makes demands on your intellect will also be very stimulating. This coupled with the added dividend of a research degree at the end of the programme makes the whole process well worth pursuing.

CHECKLIST

● Avoid entering a research programme with the attitude that you think you know all the answers before you start and all you need is to write them up into a thesis. This type of thinking only serves to keep your mind closed to new and fresh ideas.

● Ensure that you are able to reorganise your time to accommodate your research and above all make sure that you have provision for **quality thinking time**.

● Try and plan your research and fit it into a schedule. Although the schedule does not have to be rigid, you will need a time management regime otherwise the research will lose structure. Set yourself milestones and try and stick to them.

CASE STUDY

Skill updating for an electronics engineer

Gerald is an electronics engineer who has been involved in design since he graduated eight years ago. His company is moving more towards the development of digitally based systems.

Gerald feels that he needs to update his knowledge of electronics, but the university within easy travelling distance does not have a taught Master's degree in digital systems. After making a few enquiries in the Electronics Department, Gerald has ascertained that it's possible for him to register to research for an M.Phil. part-time. Having a supervisor to monitor his progress and instruct him in research techniques, Gerald will have adequate opportunity to update his skills in digital electronics.

DISCUSSION POINTS

1. What are the advantages to your company of doing an M.Phil.? Have you discussed your ideas with your employer?
2. What gaps in your knowledge might you have to fill as you embark on your research?
3. How will you set about creating quality thinking time?
4. Do you know what your intellectual limitations are?
5. Do you need to brush up on your maths?

4
Getting Involved in a Research Master's Degree

Chapter 3 looked at various general questions which you need to consider if you are thinking of studying for a research Master's degree. In this chapter we will look in more detail at certain issues relating to your proposed research.

WHAT CONSTITUTES RESEARCH?

A reasonable question to ask of any proposal is whether it is suitable for research. This is a difficult question to answer, but if your interest lies within the normal academic subject framework of a university then you stand a good chance of being accepted, albeit after some modification and rethink.

Research is not simply collecting a lot of facts and presenting them in a glossy folder – do not confuse research proper with the research used to make a television programme. Collecting information is only part of the exercise, the research proper is in the analysis and deriving new knowledge which proposes plausible answers to questions which have been hitherto unanswered.

Visiting a university

If you are invited to visit a university, take the opportunity of discussing the subject of the intended Master's programme with the members of the university's department whom you meet. Remember that if you are making a suggestion for a research proposal, you have to be realistic about the subject area – constructing scale model ships from the Second World War is not suitable. Alternatively, announcing that you've got a Pentium PC, and asking what you can do with it, will not engender a favourable response. You will probably notice that the interest shown in you by your host will suddenly evaporate. So before you visit think carefully about what you want from the visit and get your questions and proposals ready.

Pursuing your own interest

It may be that you have a broad interest in a particular subject and feel unsure as to what constitutes acceptable research. During your preliminary discussions with the academic staff this type of question will be answered. It is quite common and is usually the practice for the supervisor to propose the subject of research. They will be well aware of the current research being carried out in their specialist area and will be able to advise you accordingly. You will therefore have to be prepared to consider modifications to your proposal in the light of conversations with the academic staff. However, it is worth remembering that it's your interest in the subject that will sustain you through the duration of the research programme.

YOUR SUPERVISORS

The most important persons at the university as far as your research is concerned will be your supervisors. When you register for a research degree it is normal practice to be assigned two supervisors, one of whom you will have more frequent contact with as the principal supervisor. Unfortunately you probably won't have a choice in their selection as it is customary for research students to be allocated to supervisors by the lecturer in charge of research. In *How to Get a PhD* by Phillips and Pugh (see Further Reading) you will find a good discussion on the relationship between supervisors and research student. This is well worth reading as it will provide a valuable insight into what is expected from your supervisors and what you should and should not do as a research student.

The supervisor's role

There are a number of key points that you should always be aware of.

- You are there to learn from your supervisors and their primary teaching method will be discussions and conversation on the research you are conducting.

- They will teach you about research techniques and practices in their subject area. In order to strike up a working rapport with you, their methods of teaching are likely to be quite informal. Do not mistake this for chat, it is genuine teaching and you should be taking notes of what they are saying. They are there to guide your research and to impart their methods of thinking to you.

Inevitably there will be problems. There is likely to be a difference in intellect between you and your supervisor. Some of what they say will go straight over your head. This is not deliberate, it's just the level they think at – they have probably been working on similar problems for several years. It's up to you to point out that you don't understand the significance of what's been said. Don't just nod in agreement when you don't follow the argument – ask for more explanation.

Flagging up problems
If you don't flag a problem, your supervisors won't know. Don't be afraid to ask what may appear to be obvious questions; after all, there was a time when they didn't know either. There is no mileage in trying to look smart in front of your supervisors, as you will be the loser. Remember, it's part of their job to guide you in the ways of research and it's part of your training to learn from them.

Meetings with your supervisors
A full-time research student may see his supervisor several times a week. Spending five days a week working in the university affords close contact. Obviously, part-time students will see their supervisor less frequently. In the first eighteen months of your research you should be having meetings with your supervisor on average once every two weeks. One meeting a month is generally too infrequent. You will require close guidance during this early period and a monthly meeting is unlikely to advance your learning sufficiently. One of the main problems when you do not live within easy travelling distance of your university is maintaining regular meetings with your supervisors.

THE NATURE OF RESEARCH

There is a golden rule for every new research student, full-time or part-time:

> **Don't expect anything to be done for you. If you need anything done you must be prepared to do it yourself.**

As a research student you will do well to bear this in mind at all times. You will only progress as a result of your own application and industry.

Research techniques

Although research techniques and methodologies differ from subject to subject, they do have common patterns of application. Broadly speaking, research involves an investigation into the subject under examination. Performing research is by its nature very time-consuming and requires a considerable amount of thought. Although parts of it will be routine in its execution, much of it will require an active mind where all options are kept open.

Analysis of data

While testing, gathering data and statistics may be very repetitive and routine, their analysis and the derivation of patterns and correlations are not. In *How to Get a PhD* by Phillips and Pugh (see Further Reading) the type of research which is most appropriate for a Ph.D. is referred to as Testing-out Research. In essence, this takes existing theories or beliefs and applies them to new situations and conditions. There will already be a wealth of existing knowledge to work from. However, part of your early research will be concerned with sifting out the material that is relevant to your work. This will entail a great deal of reading and note-taking. Always make notes in your logbook of the references that you use.

Value of research

The starting point for research activity is to recognise that a subject is worthy of investigation. You may have your own idea or your supervisors will make suggestions for you. In some ways this is quite strange because they will determine what you will become an expert on through your research. If you have what you consider to be a good idea then you attach value to it and deem it worthy of investigation.

Your sense of value may be nothing more than a gut feeling or hunch that there is something interesting to investigate. Time will usually tell whether this is a useful exercise or not. The experienced researcher, your supervisors for example, will be able to give an informed opinion on the value of an idea. Many famous scientific discoveries started off as being nothing more than a *good idea at the time*. The real mystery of science is where these ideas come from in the first place.

Recognised problems

Alternatively the subject you wish to research may have been a recognised problem area which needs to be investigated in a methodical manner in order to establish a solution or finding. For example, a number of politicians would like to have hard evidence to support the supposed link between voting patterns and low taxation. You will have to determine an effective means to answer this question and what tools and techniques are needed in its investigation.

Finding out about others' research

Before you proceed any further in your plans, it is vital to find out what other workers in the field are doing. It is quite possible that the idea has occurred to someone else who has already investigated it. Although your supervisors would have informed you of this before-hand, it will be necessary to convince yourself and them that your proposed research is new.

You should be able to find this out by using the **citation indices** in the **university library**. Having discovered the state of play with regard to other research, you and your supervisor may feel that there is still a substantial amount yet to be researched.

THINKING OF VIABLE RESEARCH PROPOSALS

Before you can register as a research student at a British university it will be necessary for you to have a viable research proposal.

Full-time students

In the case of candidates for full-time research who possess a good honours degree, this is not usually a problem. Full-time research studentships are allocated to university departments for specific research proposals. If you are fortune to be accepted on one of these then you will be expected to carry out the research prescribed in the studentship contract. For example, members of staff of a university's metallurgy department may have applied to the Engineering and Physical Sciences Research Council (EPSRC) for four research student-ships relating to the strength of composite plastics. Obviously if the student awards are taken up, the research students will be expected to perform research in the prescribed areas.

Part-time students

The proposes research project may come from you or may be suggested to you by an academic member of staff in the university's department in which you hope to work.

Formulating a research proposal

From your own ideas and the suggestions of your supervisors, you will be expected to devise a coherent research proposal which will go forward to the University Research Committee (or Higher Degrees Committee or Research Degrees Committee) as part of your registration. This is an important exercise requiring a reasonable amount of effort. Ask your supervisors to comment on your drafts. If it's unacceptable the University Research Committee will expect a re-submission from you which will mean a delay in your registration – University Research Committees only sit a few times a year.

Criteria for assessing proposals

The University Research Committee will judge whether the proposal has sufficient merit to be researched and whether it is a realistic project. They will also be looking for:

● strong academic element

● originality

● evidence that you have sufficient experience and knowledge to engage in meaningful research.

The Committee will examine the strength of the proposal by referring to previous work in the field. You have to present evidence of this in your proposal. This would normally come in the form of references or previous published work that you have conducted yourself. If this is lacking, it may be concluded that you are not sufficiently knowledgeable in the subject. This will weaken your case especially if you don't possess the normal qualifications for postgraduate degree entry.

FUNDED RESEARCH

Many research studentship, leading directly to an M.Phil. or Ph.D., are funded by bodies that have a particular area or problem which needs investigating. These are normally only awarded to full-time research students or research assistants. Traditionally this has been regarded as an inexpensive way for a company to conduct research – sponsoring a research student to investigate a problem by using the facilities in the university's department. This has been particularly attractive for companies who possess limited Research & Development (R&D) facilities of their own. The type of company that sponsors this type of research is usually involved with manufacturing and product development.

Funded research for part-time research students

For a part-time student it is unlikely that sponsorship will be available except from the student's own employer. It is quite possible that you may only have support from your employer provided you conduct research which is directly relevant to them. If this is not an option you should still raise the question of funding with your supervisors. It's possible they may have knowledge of local companies who are quite prepared to offer limited assistance to part-time research students in a subject which they have an active interest in. The assistance may come in the form of university fees, a travel allowance to attend a number of conferences, or funding for software and PC peripherals.

Advantages and disadvantages

Conducting funded research has its advantages and disadvantages.

Advantages
1. The research problem has already been identified by others, *eg* a professional body which has a vested interest in having the problem investigated.
2. It is highly likely that you will have your university fees paid for you.
3. There will be funds available for the purchase of material resources such as computer peripherals and software.
4. There may even be money allocated for the attendance of conferences on closely related research fields.
5. There is a greater likelihood of a sponsored research proposal being accepted by the University Research Committee.

Disadvantages
1. The research may be in an area that you do not find particularly interesting. A strong interest in a research project is very important to sustain your momentum for the duration of the project.
2. You will have quite a rigid schedule as your sponsor will expect results by certain dates. This adds pressure to your workload which may or may not be beneficial depending how well you work under pressure.

3. You will have to write reports for your sponsor which you may regard as an unnecessary distraction from the body of your research.
4. At the end of the programme there may be insufficient material to merit a higher degree.

It is worth remembering that the needs of a sponsoring institution will be somewhat different from those of the research student. At the end of the day the institution wants results, answers to questions, whereas the research student wants enough material to merit a research degree. These two objectives are not always compatible. Follow the guidance of your supervisors, who will always act in your best interest provided you have been honest in your work.

Appendix B lists a number of institutions in the UK that sponsor postgraduate research.

Working to a schedule

One of the features of sponsored research, as mentioned above, is the need to complete certain tasks by specific dates. Although this may be anathema to your concept of research, for some the setting of deadlines by external overseers may be helpful or even necessary. This could be especially true in the early stages of a research programme when the scheduling of various tasks is necessary. Many supervisors do not impose any kind of rigid work schedule. This has led to countless full-time research students failing to complete their research in the allotted time and not submitting a thesis. The number of students failing to complete their research degrees has been a very vexing question for almost all universities in Britain.

Setting your own schedule

If you are a part-time research student it will be up to you to set your own schedule. To help you do this, it will be worth while acquiring a suitable project management software package to run on the PC; for example, **Microsoft Project** for Windows. This can be used to help you plan your work, enabling you to set your own deadlines, key events and milestones months in advance.

FILLING IN YOUR APPLICATION FORM

When you make an application to register for an M.Phil. at a university you will be expected to fill in an application form. Most of the form will be straightforward, but there will be a section where you will be expected to outline in some detail your proposed research – your **proposed plan of work**. This application, as mentioned above, will be assessed by the University Research Committee. You have to be particularly careful to present a cogent case otherwise you will be asked to resubmit your application or worst still it will be rejected.

You will find that the application form caters for three options:

1. M.Phil.
2. M.Phil. with expected transfer to Ph.D.
3. direct entry onto Ph.D.

Candidates who want to progress onto a Ph.D. programme will normally follow the second option unless they already possess a Master's degree in a relevant subject in which case they follow option 3. The nature of your proposed plan of work will depend on whether you are following options 1 or 2. If you are likely to follow option 2 your proposal will need to emphasise in some detail the research problem that you intend to investigate.

Writing your proposed plan of work

On the application form there will probably be suggestions as to the expected structure of the proposed plan of work. Members of the University Research Committee will be looking for, amongst other things, evidence of:

- a well-defined objective of the research and how you intend to tackle it; the title of the proposal should give a strong indication of the research problem

- a review of the current state of knowledge

- whether the resources are available for you to conduct your investigation

- a time plan of your proposed research.

Needs for option 2
You will be expected to focus very tightly on the research problem that you intend to investigate. This will have to be clearly defined and you will have to convince the Committee that it's a worthwhile objective and that you have the resources needed to conduct the investigation.

Needs for option 1
In this case your proposal does not have to be so highly targeted as your principal objective is to acquire research techniques and learn research practices. Nevertheless, the proposal must be sound and well argued.

Industrial and commercial links
The University Research Committee will invariably look for any industrial or commercial organisation that is involved in the research. If you (or your supervisor) can find a research problem that a company is interested in then this is likely to be viewed favourably by the Committee; for example, effects of employment law on the company's productivity, or estimating the effect of EU industrial legislation on competitiveness. It's quite conceivable that the company in question will be interested in the results of the research but is not prepared to support the programme financially. Nevertheless, such interest will still be valuable in persuading the Committee of the value of the research.

CHECKLIST

● Does the university you are interested in have a good reputation in your subject area?

● What publications have been produced by the lecturing staff in the department you are thinking of joining?

● When visiting the university, check out the research facilities that you are likely to need in the course of your research.

● Find out how well stocked the library is with periodicals in your subject area. Does the library subscribe to the well-known publications in your research area?

CASE STUDIES

Researching nineteenth-century ecumenical writings
Canon Griffiths has won the support of his bishop to research for an M.Phil. on the ecumenical writings of a nineteenth-century clergyman who influenced several important rulings of canon law.

Firstly, Canon Griffiths must find a university that has a theology department with knowledgeable experts in his chosen field. Because of the rarefied nature of his proposed research programme, it's unlikely that Canon Griffiths will find a suitable university within easy travelling distance of his parish. Secondly, he must join one of the national libraries which is likely to house much of the literature he needs access to for his research. Again this may require a fair amount of travelling. Canon Griffiths has two methods of copying the literature he requires. Obtaining a photocopy or, if funds permit, using a hand-held scanner linked to his lap-top computer to scan images of the relevant pages onto his PC's hard-disc. He must plan his time carefully, visiting his university for supervision and visiting the appropriate libraries for literature.

Pursuing an M.Phil. to enhance promotion opportunities

Bernadette has been working in the County Surveyor's office for five years and is seeking promotion as a Land Commissioner. She has been told, unofficially, that a Master's degree together with her experience would make her more attractive for promotion in what is predominantly a male preserve.

Bernadette lives within easy travelling distance of a new university that has a well-known geography department. Unfortunately they do not run a taught Master's degree programme. After discussions with the head of department, Bernadette has been invited to submit an application to do research leading to an M.Phil. She had been informed what specialists exist within the department and has been advised to keep the theme of her research within the expertise of the department. She has also been asked to present ideas of her own before any suggestions are made by members of the lecturing staff.

- She needs to begin by thinking of several ideas that she could investigate. At this stage the ideas should be quite specific, possibly reflecting her own interests and real problems that she has encountered in her job.

- She must be careful not to be too ambitious in her proposed research. If Bernadette proposes a programme that is unrealistic in terms of timescale or her own ability, this will indicate that she has little understanding of the task and will be judged as not being suitable material for an M.Phil. programme.

- Likewise if she chooses a problem that is trivial, then again she will be considered to be unsuitable for a research programme.

- Ideally, the ideas that Bernadette proposes should have foundations in well-researched or established practices. It is upon these practices that she can build her own suggestions – look at what other people have done and take it further.

Using findings, established while working, as material for an M.Phil.

Brian is a software engineer and has been working for several years on designing methods of distributing and accessing databases over a network of computers. He has come up with several new methodologies and is wondering if he can submit his findings as viable research for an M.Phil. degree.

The answer is probably yes. These days many universities will give backdating credit (normally six months, but this could be longer in exceptional circumstances). Although Brian's minimum time to submission can be reduced, he still has to go through a formal scheme of requirements for an M.Phil. research programme. What Brian has to do is find a suitable university, within easy travelling distance, and discuss his research proposal with a lecturer in its computer science department who has an expertise in the subject area of distributed databases.

DISCUSSION POINTS

1. Make a list of possible subject areas that fall within your expertise and discuss with knowledgeable friends or colleagues the merits of your ideas.
2. What is the specific nature of the research you are proposing to undertake? What research techniques will you be using? How will you plan your work?
3. See if you can find, in your place of employment, anyone else who possesses an M.Phil. degree and discuss with them how they got through the programme.

5
Using the University's Resources

Every British university will have numerous resources and your use of them will depend largely upon the subject you are reading. Science and engineering-based Master's programmes tend to have more laboratory work than the Humanities. Therefore students pursuing a science or engineering degree will be expected to develop new **laboratory skills**. These take time and it's likely that a fair amount of your time will be spent in the laboratory.

Bear in mind that the PC has now become a familiar tool in all laboratories, whether in chemistry, biology, engineering or physics. It is very likely that you will be expected to develop **PC skills** as part of the Master's programme.

The **library** is also an important resource and it will be a valuable exercise to find out as soon as possible what the library has to offer.

USING THE LABORATORY

The student on a Master's degree programme in science or engineering will be expected to spend a fair amount of time performing laboratory exercises in order to acquire the necessary practical skills for the subject being studied. You will find that whatever science or engineering Master's degree programme you are on their will be sufficient laboratory resources provided for you – otherwise the university would not run the course.

The time spent in the laboratory will be in addition to the time spent in lectures and tutorials. Part-time students will be required to commit a day a week or at least half a day a week and some of this time will be spent in the lab.

Many laboratory skills now rely on a proficiency in the use of personal computers, so be prepared to learn new skills here too. There are several software packages available for plotting data and presenting it in an acceptable format. The days of hand-plotted data using graph paper are numbered. If you are not already familiar with

linear regression it may be well worth reading up on the subject before you start your Master's degree programme. Several PC software packages (**Mathcad**, for example – see Chapter 9) will perform regression analysis for you, but you still need an understanding of what it's doing.

Your laboratory logbook

When you start the course you will be provided with information regarding the use of your laboratory logbook. A logbook should be a hard-cover A4 exercise book preferably with graph paper on alternate pages. It is a very important asset and you should make sure that you keep an accurate record of everything you do in the lab – **date every entry**. Your logbook may even form part of your assessment and it will therefore be in your interest to keep it up to date.

READING ACADEMIC MATERIAL

The primary source of information is the textbook and every subject has a wealth of publications dealing with virtually all its aspects. There are, however, two problems related to textbooks, the first is that of dating and the second is cost.

Presentation methods change and subjects advance. Although a lot of knowledge is carried from successive generations of textbooks, the style and subject emphasis changes. Extreme examples of redundancy are found in computer books, which are severely affected by changes in technology – the flavour of today will be old hat tomorrow (or sooner). For example, a book written on a software product or a particular type of PC hardware has a useful life of two years at most.

The problem of redundancy in book stocks is seriously affecting university libraries. Textbooks are expensive for what they are and are suffering high unnatural inflation rates because they are sourced in the USA. At the same time the finance allocated to university libraries is being cut back. The newly registered Master's student will probably find the library somewhat under-stocked and what stock does exist will appear to be well past its sell-by date.

Background reading

During your preliminary discussion with your supervisors they will suggest a number of textbooks to read in order to get you started on the subject. As a matter of course you should try and get hold of every textbook on the recommended reading list issued with each module. Textbooks should provide you with a sufficient background knowledge to enable you to complement the knowledge imparted by the lecturers during the tutorials and lectures.

Difficulties in reading textbooks

Surprisingly few people can read technical literature without experiencing problems. This is abundantly evident from the little attention that is given to Owner's Manuals of new equipment. One of the main complaints from the technical help-line of many companies, is that when customers ring up with a problem, the information they seek is in the Owner's Manual and it's quite obvious that the customer hasn't read it. If you are not accustomed to reading textbooks or technical literature then you may come across three types of problem.

Problem 1: Difficulty in sustaining a good reading pattern
The first symptom of this condition is the wandering of the mind onto other matters while you are reading something which is difficult to understand. This could be due to the fact that, as yet, you have not acquired the reading skills necessary to maintain your concentration – your **attention span** is too short.

Solution
This condition has been recognised and is well known, especially among American publishers. In many computer textbooks, which originate from America, you will never find a page of solid print. Each page is broken up into small paragraphs and one of the margins will be wide. Parts of the text will be highlighted to make the page more attractive for the purpose of sustaining the reader's interest. Different colours are also used for the same purpose. You will also find the liberal use of clip-art figures.

By supplying information in small batches, there is a greater chance that the reader's concentration is maintained for a longer period. It's a question of stringing together a sequence of short attention spans to achieve long duration attention. If you have problems with short attention spans, try reading an American textbook on an aspect of PCs that you find interesting – read it from cover to cover. The more you read technical literature the greater your sustaining power will become.

Problem 2: Failure to recognise the overall linkage in an argument
This difficulty relates to the failure to understand the collective linkage between a set of facts which constitute an argument. To illustrate this

condition we can consider a teaching example: when explaining a mathematical derivation with steps 1 to 10, a student can understand steps 1 to 2, and from steps 2 to 3 through to steps 9 to 10. But when asked, can't understand collective steps 1 to 10 which incorporate all of the intervening steps. Although they understand all the individual steps they find difficulty in integrating this knowledge to generate a complete understanding of steps 1 to 10. They understand the individual facts but are unable to appreciate their collective significance.

Solution
The first step needed to correct this condition is to recognise it. During your preparatory and background reading you will come across complex arguments and you will be confronted with just such a dilemma. If after several readings the argument still evades you and doesn't make sense, although you understand parts of it, try and break down the argument into its individual parts and sort out the **causes**, the **effects**, the **ifs** and the **thens**. One of the problems with the written word is that of clarity. What appears to be clear to the author is not shared by all the readers. It is at times like these that discussions with your supervisor will be useful. Having another perspective on the argument usually clarifies the issues and enhances the level of understanding.

Problem 3: Not being able to skim-read efficiently
This problem arises from reading too much detail and not being able to appreciate the salient points of the argument. **Skim-reading** is quite an art and its purpose is to allow you to read through a passage and ascertain whether it contains anything of relevance for your subject.

Solution
To acquire the skill of effective skim-reading you must rid yourself of the habit of **sub-vocalising** – reading the words in your mind. This is an unnecessary hindrance to the reading process. The objective is to look at a word and recognise its meaning without having to read it, in the same way that when you see an object such as a door, you do not say to yourself 'door' because you recognise it for what it is. By dispensing with the sub-vocalising process, your reading speed can be increased by a factor of ten. One method of achieving this is by reading (viewing) text faster than you can sub-vocalise it. Tony Buzan has written a useful book on *Speed Reading* which is worth consulting if you have these problems (see Further Reading).

USING THE LIBRARY

In all disciplines the library is a major resource centre for all research projects. The quality of university libraries varies across the country. The traditional universities tend to have the best libraries in terms of stock because their needs have been somewhat different from the new universities. However, since there is a convergence in higher education the expectation of both the new and traditional universities libraries are the same. The main resources of a university library fall into the following groups:

- **Books.** The first and foremost resource of any library. Because of the changing nature of knowledge, books are upgraded regularly and this requires the greatest expenditure. Library books are useful to refer to, but books recommended by the lecturers should be bought by the student. You cannot rely on the library to make available to you for the duration of a module the recommended reading. Other students will require the books and it's likely that even if the library has several copies of a book there will be restrictions on the loan time.

- **Journals.** The principal means of making known to the public the results of research is through the journal. Every discipline has several journals dedicated to it and sometimes it is appropriate for students on Master's programmes to refer to these journals (see further below). Every university library will have a limited selection of journals – they are a very expensive asset to maintain.

- **Interlibrary loans.** A scheme to borrow books or obtain copies of articles from other sources or libraries (see further below).

- **Video tapes.** An important learning aid especially for under-graduate courses (see further below).

- **PC data.** Many libraries have networked PCs which have access to citation indices – juke-boxes of CD-ROMs carrying research data and information on publications in general.

- **Online services.** It is now commonplace for university libraries to have direct contact with a number of online computer services to enable researchers to gain access to a broader range of information sources.

- **CD-ROMs.** Much of today's new information and knowledge is stored on CD-ROMs which can be accessed by a PC hosting a CD-ROM drive. University libraries subscribe to a number of companies and institutions which provide information on CD-ROMs. The information covers a whole range of academic subjects and you should make enquiries with the subject librarian to determine what information is available on CD-ROM (see further below).

All university libraries have to work within limited resources and the problem is not getting any easier, so don't be surprised to find that the more obscure journals or editions of books are not stocked by the library. A student's understanding of the difficulties that library staff have to work with will be much appreciated.

Journals

Textbooks are useful for providing the necessary background material to strengthen your previously acquired knowledge of your subject. However, the research starts in earnest with the journals that contain the recently published work and advances in your field.

All publications (or papers) in academic journals are **refereed** by an acknowledged expert in the field. If the referee is of the opinion that the paper submitted has something original to announce and is worthy of publication then usually the journal will accept it.

At the end of each paper there will be a number of **references to other publications** on the same subject.

Reading journal articles

As a research student you will be expected to read the relevant journals. You will find that the style of writing of papers in most journals is not as rounded as found in textbooks.

The authors of papers are expected to be very concise with no unnecessary description or discussion of their subject matter. This does not bode too well for the new research student who has enough difficulties reading textbooks where the style is much freer and usually more descriptive. You simply have to persevere with the paper until it makes sense. Don't forget to involve your supervisor – if you have difficulties then he/she is there for you to ask. Reading research papers and mastering their content is part of the learning process of acquiring research expertise.

Other publications

Your university library will also subscribe to many trade journals, magazines and other publications which do not fall under the description of refereed journal. These too are valuable sources of information and tend to be much easier going for the reader, with the writing style much freer and more descriptive. To attract the interest of the reader the articles are well supported by diagrams which add a visual element.

These general interest journals or magazines tend to dwell on the interesting developments in a subject as opposed to detailed research findings. Development usually emerges from successful research; what you read in today's trade journals and magazines is the implementation of research carried out previously.

Citation indices

During your introduction to the resources in the library you will be introduced to the **citation indices**. As a new researcher in a specific field you will be expected to become familiar with the other research carried out. Part of your research is to ascertain whether your proposed research project has been tackled by anyone else. By looking in the citation indices you will be able to identify other papers that have been written on your subject. After each entry in the citation indices there will be a list of other publications which have referenced it. The classic publications are usually referred to by most of the subsequent publications on the subject, and this will help you to pick out those papers which are essential for you to read.

Citation indices on CD-ROMs

Your university library may have the citation indices on CD-ROM which will make the task of listing the citations somewhat easier. Otherwise you will have to refer to the written versions. The next task is to get photocopies of the articles listed in the citations.

Photocopying research papers

Fortunately there is no copyright restriction on academic papers from learned journals provided only one copy is made for the purposes of study or research. If you are lucky your university library may have the journals cited in the indices and it's an easy task to just photocopy the papers. As a research student you will soon find your collection of photocopied papers growing as you try and gather all the information on your research topic. **Photocopying papers is not the same as reading them.** It is good practice to read the papers as soon as you get the photocopies of them. Storing them away for another time is like the collection of television programmes you have on video that you haven't watched yet – many of them months old.

Interlibrary loans

With the cash shortages which are affecting many university libraries you should not be surprised to find that your library does not stock all the journals which are referred to in the citations. However, you will find that the library operates an interlibrary loan scheme which will enable a photocopy of the required paper to be bought in from another library which has the journal. Although a very useful service, the problem is that you have to wait about a fortnight for the copy to come through. The interlibrary loan scheme also accommodates the loan of textbooks, but there will be a problem if the required book is in great demand elsewhere.

Video tapes

Most university libraries will have a collection of video tapes and televisions to watch them on. This resource is normally used for undergraduate teaching, but it might be in your interest to attend some undergraduate lectures to brush up on a particular aspect relating to your field of research. Your supervisor will advise on this. If you are lucky, the lecturer who normally gives the lectures has committed them to video tape. You will then be at liberty to view them at your leisure within the confines of the library.

CD-ROMs and the library

With the millions of books published one effective of way of keeping a catalogue of them is to use the medium of the CD-ROM. Every university library will have this facility and they will subscribe to a cataloguing company or institution which produces book lists on CD-ROMs. With the rapid growth in publishing it is important for the information to be updated regularly. This is usually the case and the CD-ROMs are replaced on average four times a year. There will of course be other CD-ROMs referring to different types of publications.

When you join the library you will be presented with a list of the resources and services that the library has to offer. Look carefully at the section relating to Information Technology and how it has been incorporated into the library to provide a comprehensive service to its users. **Chadwyck Healey** from Cambridge, Tel: (01223) 215512, is famous for publishing academic material on CD-ROM and they publish an annual catalogue of their range of educational products.

USING THE COMPUTER CENTRE

It is highly likely that the **computer centre** at the university will not only have mainframe (such as ICL 1690) or minicomputers (such as a VAX) but also a suite of networked PCs. As a registered student, even part-time, if required you will be issued with access rights onto the PC network and the mainframe. You will then have the opportunity of trying out the software available on the network. These will include standard wordprocessors, spreadsheets, databases and probably statistical and mathematical modelling software. It is quite possible that you will find some of the software in the computer centre suitable for your research. If this is the case try to get your department to buy a copy at a special educational discounted rate.

PC facilities

There will be other facilities in the computer centre that you should be using, such as printers, image scanners and the CD-ROM library. However, you must not neglect the remote access services offered by the centre. The computer centre will also have access points to the **Superhighway** or **Internet** which gives you the opportunity of reaching a vast array of international databases. You may encounter some restriction on the time allocated for **surfing the net** because this service is not free and the university is expected to pay for it. Use your access time wisely.

CHECKLIST

- When you register at a university make sure that you are issued with a set of regulations for:

  1. the library
  2. the computer centre
  3. laboratory practice (if appropriate).

- Also make sure that you are issued with a Recommended Reading List (RRL) for the modules that you will be pursuing in the first term (or semester).

- If you are following a science Master's programme find out what computer software you will be required to use or learn and whether there are any books in the library on it.

CASE STUDIES

Master's degree in education
David is about to start a Master's degree in education and has a particular interest in the use of computers in secondary education.

The use of computers in education, at all levels, has become a subject of intense interest over the last few years. Although the degree course David is registered on covers many aspects of education management, it would be in David's interest to make 'Computer Learning Methods in Education' the theme of his Master's dissertation. He will need to find out what published material is available on this subject. David's course of action is therefore as follows:

- Access the citation indices in the university library and perform database search operations on the words 'computers' and 'secondary education'.

- On receiving a list of publications from his search, select the publications that are likely to be of interest.

- If the publications are not available in the library, ask the appropriate library services for interlibrary loans on the books and/or copies of the papers.

Master's programme in economic modelling
Elizabeth has registered on a Development Economics Master's degree, and has been informed that it will require a fair amount of statistics and modelling.

The majority of statistical and modelling calculations are performed on PCs and Elizabeth should ascertain either from the university's computer centre or from the admissions tutor the software packages used on the degree programme. Elizabeth should then:

- Perform a search, using the university's library facilities, to determine whether there are any books published on the application of the software to economics.

- If she finds any books listed, determine whether they are on the Recommended Reading List (RRL) for the degree.

- Determine whether the library carries stock of them (if they are on the RRL they will be stocked) and their respective loan period.

- If they are not on the RRL and the library does not stock them, consider visiting a good bookshop to inspect them – ringing the shop first to ensure they are in stock.

Using information on CD-ROMs in a Master's degree

Martin, having registered on an Analytical Chemistry Master's programme, wants to know what information is available on CD-ROM which would be useful for his degree.

Martin's first point of enquiry would be the university library where he would ask about the online services and whether there are any databases of chemical data available on CD-ROM. In particular Martin could ask about:

- Dictionaries from **Chapman & Hall** on:

  1. analytical reagents
  2. inorganic compounds
  3. organic compounds.

- **Kirk-Othmer** Encyclopaedia of Chemical Technology. Although these CD-ROMs are too expensive for an individual to buy, access might be available though the library computer system. It is customary to have CD-ROMs stored in a **juke-box** peripheral attached to the computer system.

DISCUSSION POINTS

1. What type of facilities would you expect a university to make available to you for your chosen subject?
2. If you are likely to pursue a part-time Master's degree, what type of help and technical support can you expect from your place of employment?
3. Do you need to improve your reading skills?

6
Looking at an MBA

Over the past ten years Master of Business Administration (MBA) degrees have become very popular. There are over one hundred MBA courses on offer from British institutions and over 6,700 students are taking them. In many universities the MBA course is run as part of the university curriculum whereas other institutions keep their MBAs quite separate; for example, University of Oxford School of Management and the London Business School. Several universities also run M.Sc. programmes in business administration, where there is generally greater emphasis on the dissertation part of the degree. (See the Further Reading section for sources of information on MBAs.)

WHY DO AN MBA DEGREE?

There is a growing feeling that being in possession of an MBA degree is no bad thing. This belief has arisen from a wealth of anecdotal evidence suggesting that an MBA degree is a passport to a high-profile job with matching salary. To many this has been true as illustrated by the median salary commanded by holders of the degree which is around £49,000. Certainly if you are interested in improving your job opportunities or hoping to change career, an MBA would be one choice to consider. Increasing your earning potential is obviously a compelling reason for wanting to pursue an MBA programme. However, with the apparent popularity of MBAs it is quite possible that an oversupply may dampen some prospects. This factor should be considered in the light of the expense of gaining an MBA degree.

Finding a course

MBAs are available in a number of formats, full-time, part-time and through distance learning, the last of these being very attractive if you cannot get remission from your employment. To find out which best suits your needs write to the universities that run MBA courses. Most British universities run such courses and it would be very surprising if there wasn't one within relatively easy travelling distance of your home. However, if you are a fresh graduate (under 26) it is unlikely that you will be able to secure a position on an MBA programme. Most institutions insist that candidates should have a number of years working after graduating before commencing an MBA degree.

Admission tests

Candidates for MBA degrees come from diverse backgrounds and it's not uncommon for institutions to use the Official Guide for the Graduate Management Admission Test (GMAT), which contains in excess of 900 exercises, to measure a candidate's suitability for entry onto an MBA programme. The *GMAT Review* is available from **Pastest**, Tel: (01565) 755226.

Part-time MBAs

It is customary for part-time MBA programmes to last two years and the nature of course should complement your current employment. When pursuing a part-time MBA programme you have the advantages of remaining within employment with no need to suffer long periods away from your work. It therefore does not interrupt your career progression. In fact, on its completion, your career prospects should be greatly enhanced. The skills you acquire on an MBA programme can be applied immediately to the benefit of your employer – your justification for obtaining financial support becomes apparent. You will also have the opportunity to meet like-minded people with work experience from disparate environments, thus allowing the exchange of ideas.

Group discussions

If you already hold a managerial position it's likely that you will use your current state of knowledge to contribute to group discussion on problem-solving. It's not unusual to have alternative solutions debated in a group environment where each candidate argues the strengths of their methodology when applied to case study exercises. This, in itself, is regarded as an important means of self-development and of enhancing personal confidence.

LOOKING AT COURSE FORMATS

A typical MBA programme will have a modular structure and each module will be given over the duration of one term. Several modules will be given each term. Although the nature of MBA programmes

will vary from university to university, typically you should expect
to find a variety of modules covering the current thinking in business
management and administration.

Accounting

This will include **financial** and **management** accounting. Financial
accounting deals with balance sheets, profit and loss, cash flow,
accrual accounting, stock value (its depreciation), fixed assets, business transactions, preparing final accounts, auditing and interpreting
financial statements. Management accounting deals mainly with
budgeting and costing, including product costing, overhead assessment, marginal and absorption costing techniques and incremental
cost analysis. There should also be discussion on divisional performance as profit centres and return on investment and residual income.

Marketing

Dealing with the planning, implementation and control of marketing
strategies, this module will probably include the means of developing
long-term relationships with customers through a culture of trust. The
significance of marketing concepts must be appreciated and emphasis
will probably be placed on the importance of product and/or service
quality, effect of price variations, promotional activity and the
geography of service/product distribution. As part of any organisation, consideration will be given to the financing of marketing
strategies and techniques for measuring their effectiveness.

Strategic management

This type of module is intended to impart to managers analytical skills
to enable them to review complex organisational problems with the
objective of predicting the outcomes of their strategies. Material
in the module will dwell on the nature of strategic competitive
advantages and how they are analysed in the context of a company's
development. You should also find discussions on value chains and
systems, stake-holders and generic strategies. These will be considered
within the context of industrial structures and their inherent culture.
Having looked at the techniques for devising strategies you should
be taught the various means for effective implementation. By using
sensitivity analysis you should be able to predict best and worst case
scenarios for small-scale and large-scale businesses of introducing new
management strategies.

Financial management

This module will deal with the allocation, funding and management of resources in an organisation. It considers stock management and financial forecasting in the short term and long term, the identification of incremental effects of investment and methods of determining profitability and discounted cash flow. This should include risk and uncertainty and its practical consideration. Long-term financial management looks at debt and equity capital and reviews methods of making equity issues and divident policies. Capital costs and the gains of mergers and acquisitions should also be analysed.

Business economics

This module will probably be divided into micro and macro-economics, the former dealing with consumer behaviour affecting demand, costs and production decisions. Also considered should be an analysis of the determination of pricing policy, the influence of the distribution of income and how markets fail due to social effects and external political events. Macroeconomics will deal with the role of government in the management of the economy and its effect on national income. Also included should be discussions on:

- monetary policy and interest rates
- the effects of growth on demand and the nature of supply economics
- international influences via the money markets and exchange rates
- inflation and its effect on employment.

It is probable that the module will also include a discussion of the Keynesian approach to aggregate demand in the economy in general. A sound understanding of these principles greatly facilitates one's understanding of financial management, production and marketing appreciation.

Human resource development

Themes covered in this module will include the management of people in an organisation, improving personnel management skills, developing team and group environments and analysing the management dynamics of organisations. Stress should be placed on the importance of group motivation, system dynamics and team-building. This will probably be done in the context of organisational culture incorporating change and management development. Reviewing industrial relations and related issues will probably figure in this module.

Project management

Many companies compete in an aggressive marketplace where deadlines, delivery schedules and critical service demands are paramount. By defining these provisions within a project framework, they can be expertly managed provided appropriate managerial skills are exercised. Project management skills enable an effective project manager to maintain a global overview of a product or service development. Thus an appropriate module will impart an understanding of project planning and scheduling, progress analysis, risk management, role definition and means for judging project success or failure. An integral part of such a module will be techniques for effective people management.

Management information and systems

Information technology and information systems (IS) now form a vital management resource and a sound understanding of its strategic role is essential for an effective manager. Typically you would expect in this module an in-depth appreciation of how ISs provide multi-functional services within a company, how to prioritise the services for the more information-intensive demands, and extending the range of services as technology advances. Emphasis should also be placed on the importance of including IS development within global organisational planning. This will include the definition of a manager's role in IS implementation schemes and the nature of its management in order to optimise managerial performance.

Quantitative methods and analysis

The ability to perform analysis on management problems using quantitative techniques is an essential skill that all effective managers should possess. This type of module should therefore introduce you to the various techniques, implemented on personal computers, for analysis purposes. It should provide you with a wide variety of tools for performing statistical analysis. These will probably include the analysis of risk, sensitivity and uncertainty, significance testing and multiple regression and forecasting. To benefit from this type of module you will be expected to have a reasonable grasp of mathematics.

Operations management

This is concerned with the provision and management of physical resources within an organisation to fulfil client needs for products and/or services while maintaining a rigid cost discipline. In order to effect an optimum operations management regime, a complete knowledge is required of how storage and production capacity, throughput rate, quality management, process design and customer delivery lead-times integrate into a coherent system. This module should therefore cover the various management tools required to carry out performance and sensitivity analysis. The cost-effectiveness of just-in-time (JIT) should also be included allowing you to judge its appropriateness for a particular company's operations.

Specialist modules

The above list of modules is by no means exhaustive but should serve as an indication of what to expect in an MBA course whether it is full-time, part-time or delivered in any other mode. Several institutions offer a range of elective modules which will reflect your particular interest. Other modules may deal with a variety of subjects, for example:

- corporations and multinationals
- international strategies
- global business environments
- strategic planning for tiger economics
- understanding European law and management styles.

By consulting the MBA prospectus from the university that interests you, you will probably see the complete list on offer. Although the modules discussed in this chapter are quite general, several universities offer specialised MBA programmes; for example, Cranfield University offers a European Human Resource Management MBA and a Public Sector MBA.

EXAMINING CASE STUDIES METHODS

The majority of MBA programmes place heavy emphasis on the significance of case studies. This is to be expected as much of the accumulated knowledge relating to business administration is derived from actual experience and the practical implementation of management strategies. Case study analysis is a powerful technique for teaching and developing problem-solving skills. By working through case studies you become accustomed to making decisions, implementing them and convincing others of the merits of your actions. The process of case study analysis can be subdivided into the following three phases:

Case history assimilation

By reading through the case study documentation you will assimilate the salient features of its development and prepare yourself for further discussion and analysis. The more facts you can remember the better equipped you will be in the second and third phase of the analysis.

Group discussion

By expanding your understanding of your perception of the case study you have the opportunity to persuade others, in a small group, of the strengths of your management proposals. You will also hear from others in the group where you will be able to accept or reject alternative strategies to your own. You will also be able to modify your own solutions in view of the alternative strategies.

Full group presentation

By the time you have reached this stage, you will have formulated your management strategy for the case study and you will invariably meet with opposition from other fervent-minded managers who intend to adopt different strategies to your own. You therefore have the opportunity to stand your ground and push through the decisions that you've adopted. This will require persuasion, tact and ability to work under pressure. Performing in a large group of people, several of whom may be equally determined to force through their views, is no mean task. It's quite possible that their strategies make more sense than yours, so do you continue to argue the merits of your own or make concessions to others? Case studies have no unique solutions, and it will therefore be up to you to argue the merits of your solutions. Either way the whole exercise should be an effective means of developing confidence.

CONSIDERING ASSESSMENT METHODS

In general, modules will be assessed in a number of ways, depending upon the university. Assessment methods may include:

- examinations at the end of the term
- written assignments

- presentation performance
- case study performance
- dissertation.

These methods of assessment are discussed in more detail in Chapters 2 and 10 and it's important that you familiarise yourself with the do's and don'ts of each. Discuss the various assessment methods with your lecturers – this is especially true for the assignments to ensure that you provide what is expected.

Dissertation

The all-important dissertation project may relate to a real consultancy problem drawn from an industrial or commercial organisation. While not all institutions require a dissertation as part of their assessment, if you are accepted at a university that does require one, make sure that you enter into early discussion with your supervisor and enquire about the dissertation, its depth of coverage, its format and the weighting allocated to it.

MBA THROUGH DISTANCE LEARNING

Much of what is said in Chapter 7 relating to Master's degrees by distance learning (DL) is equally relevant to the MBA DL programmes. A number of British institutions offer MBAs in a distance learning format, including:

- the Open University
- University of Durham
- University of Kingston
- University of Warwick
- Heriot-Watt University
- University of Strathclyde
- Henley Management College.

Success in a DL MBA will depend upon your personal motivation. As in other DL programmes, you will have an opportunity to meet other candidates on the course during summer school gatherings.

ASSOCIATION OF MBAS

As in many other walks of professional life, there is an association that monitors and accredits MBA courses for standards. Known as the **Association of MBAs** (AMBA), this body acts as a quality monitor for MBA courses in the UK and usually considers the institution's reputation for research and how well they attract research funding. More information on the role of the AMBA and the institutions they accredit can be obtained from their central office (Tel: (0171) 837 3375).

HOW MUCH WILL IT COST?

It must be stressed that MBAs are expensive by comparison with other Master's degrees. For example, the distance learning course from the Open University costs almost £8,000. Likewise the full-time fees for an MBA course at Warwick are £10,000. Depending on the institution the duration of a full-time MBA programme may be one or two years and other programmes may take as long as four years part-time. Because they are expensive, you must feel very confident that it will benefit you before you embark on such a programme.

Getting financial support

It's unlikely that you will get a bursary to pursue an MBA programme as the majority of MBA students are already in full-time employment. You may be very lucky and work for a company that has an active policy for advancing employee skills and is prepared to support you for the duration of the course. The government operates a **Career Development Loan** (CDL) scheme and will advance you a loan of up to £8,000. However, you have to begin repayment one month after the course has finished, or if you are unemployed you can defer the repayment for six months. Details can be obtained from Barclays, Co-operative or Clydesdale banks which participate in the scheme.

There is also an **AMBA Business School Loan Scheme** from the Association of MBAs. To qualify for a loan you must first secure a place on an MBA course at an AMBA accredited institution and be a permanent resident of the UK. Again details of this loan are available from the participating banks. If you are over 30 you may be eligible for tax relief on the course fees.

CHECKLIST

- Before you make any plans for applying for an MBA course, carefully work through the finances of the project.

- Ask your employer whether they are likely to support you on an

MBA programme. If not, ask whether they are prepared to loan you the money for the course.

● Make a realistic assessment of whether the MBA will be regarded as a sound career development and therefore help you get a better paid job.

● Obtain from the Association of MBAs a list of accredited institutions.

CASE STUDIES

Enhancing your job prospects with a Master's degree

Kathleen joined a famous supermarket store ten years ago after graduating in English and has progressed to a senior managerial position. However, she feels that her skills need updating if she is to make any further progress in the company.

This is a condition that confronts many managers in their early to mid-thirties. Provided Kathleen can secure a position to an MBA programme, which is highly likely in view of her experience after graduating, she will have the choice of pursuing the MBA part-time or full-time. This will depend on her personal circumstances with regard to her family and her current workload. If she lives within easy travelling distance of a university, it may be in her interest to consider a part-time programme. Kathleen will have to weigh up very carefully the effect of taking on the extra workload of a Master's programme and how it will affect her employment and her family.

Skill updating for a project manager

Geoffrey has been working as a project manager for a defence company since he graduated in production engineering. Now in his late twenties, he needs a skill updating programme to make him more effective as a project manager.

Firstly Geoffrey should ascertain whether the defence company he works for will support him on a full-time MBA programme. As a project manager Geoffrey may have more than one project on the boil at any one time. Before he embarks on a full-time MBA programme he needs to bring them to a close at the same time or pass them onto someone else. Once a project has been completed or is passed onto another phase, for example, from development to production, Geoffrey would normally be assigned a new project. This is a convenient juncture to take time out to do an MBA programme. He should also try to find an MBA programme that caters for his special needs as a production manager.

Investing your redundancy money in an MBA

Edith has recently been made redundant after ten years of employment. Still in her thirties, Edith was given a very generous golden handshake and is wondering whether to spend it on an MBA course.

Edith's course of action will depend on several factors, including:

- Whether she was a well-paid manager before she was made redundant (more than £40,000 a year).

- Whether she already has children.

- What her husband thinks of the idea.

- Whether the possession of an MBA will help her get a better paid job than she had previously.

- Whether she should be applying for new jobs now instead of thinking about an MBA.

- Whether a part-time MBA programme would be more appropriate to her needs and how far she would have to travel.

- If she does decide to do an MBA, how long it would take after she resumes working (assuming she gets another well-paid managerial position) to claw back the money spent on the course.

- Whether she would like a complete change in career direction not involving management. Should she be thinking of investing in a Master's degree in another subject?

Edith has several decisions to make. It could be argued that her most appropriate course of action would be to continue looking for another job and if nothing is forthcoming then consider spending her own money on an MBA course.

DISCUSSION POINTS

1. Discuss with your spouse the costs that would be incurred in doing an MBA. Make realistic estimates.

2. Discuss with your line manager and the personnel director at work what advantages there would be if you had an MBA.

3. Also discuss with them whether an MBA programme is considered as a desirable career or staff development exercise.

7
Looking at Distance Learning Master's Degrees

Distance learning (DL) has become an attractive option for many Master's degree programmes. The idea of open learning has been around for several years and has now been extended to create a DL means to facilitate higher education. Many universities offer DL programmes as alternatives to conventional learning modes. The advent of multimedia PC has greatly facilitated the move towards DL schemes. The principal learning method of the Open University has been DL and this has proved to be extremely successful over the past twenty-five years. Although the OU has the luxury of a television channel and various radio channels to disseminate its information, traditional universities have to rely on other means. No doubt when digital television broadcasting comes on stream this situation will change and most universities will have their own television channel.

There is also a Web site on the Internet that offers some information on DL. It's located at:

```
http://www.distance-learning.co.uk
```

REVIEWING PERSONAL COMMITMENT

Clearly, when working from a DL programme, the student will be expected to manage their own time in a very well-disciplined manner. In traditional teaching methods, students learn within a rigid framework. They have a schedule and are expected to conform to it. The lonely DL student must set their own schedule and keep to it. This may be very difficult especially when family commitments make uneven demands on their time.

When you first register on a DL Master's degree programme you will be assigned a **personal tutor** or **supervisor** who will take a personal interest in your progress. It's important that you keep them informed of any problems that you encounter during the course.

Watch out for slippage

Normally the DL programme will be partitioned into weekly tasks that the student will be expected to complete on time. It is vitally important that you keep to the schedule laid down by the programme designers. If problems arise they must be flagged up with your course tutor as soon as possible.

Don't rely on holidays to catch up

Many students, who are expected to manage their own time regarding a project or a learning pattern, experience slippage. Their solution, 'I can catch up over Christmas or Easter', never works. All it needs for the programme to come to a dead halt is for the student to encounter one aspect of the subject they don't understand or don't have sufficient information about to continue. Problems are usually difficult to predict and it's only when you work through your material that you are able to appreciate its significance.

Tutors are not normally available over the holiday period and generally resent having their holiday disturbed by students who have failed to manage their time properly. As a DL student experiencing slippage, you may choose to use up some of your holiday entitlement to catch up, only to find that your tutor is not available.

Employment support

DL is a very effective means of extending your knowledge base through a programme of structured study. Although the work programme is flexible it does require a high degree of self-discipline. However, you may be able to obtain support from your employer, who may even pay for the programme should it become an acceptable part of your company's skill updating scheme.

LOOKING AT STUDY MATERIAL

The material needed by the student to pursue a DL course will vary depending on the nature of the Master's programme. The programme may have a high learning requirement which is common with a science or engineering degree. Alternatively with a Humanities programme, the material may require a high level of discussion. Typically a DL Master's programme may consist of the following:

- written text
- reference books and articles
- video tapes

- computer software
- interactive CD-ROMs.

Before a university launches a Master's degree through DL it's likely that they will have run it previously in another mode (full-time or part-time). It's usually from the previous experience that the material for the DL programme is drawn.

Written text

This will invariably be a lecturer's notes presented in a coherent and readable format. A lecturer's notes are usually a skeleton of the material that is presented during a lecture. By adding the meat to the skeleton, the notes are transformed into a complete information source that the DL student can learn from directly. It is likely that the written texts will be supplemented by problems and even solutions.

Reference books and articles

As every student knows, the material of a lecture course must be supplemented by additional reading from recognised sources. This is especially true for DL students since they have to depend, to a great deal, on their own learning processes to acquire information and the analysis tools for understanding the course material. A number of universities will provide the standard textbooks required for further reading. Articles will also be supplied as these are frequently used as valuable source material.

Video tapes

Video tapes can be a valuable means of disseminating lecture material. Some universities have lecture studios for recording lectures and it is not exceptional to find video tapes of lectures in the university library. While the lecture is in progress, the video editor can use several video cameras at the same time to ensure that all the material is recorded and emphasised, although more editing can be performed at a later date.

It has often been said that one of the problems of watching a video of a lecture as opposed to attending a lecture is the lack of opportunity for asking questions. Surprising as it may seem, relatively few questions are ever asked during a lecture anyway, so in many cases this should not be a problem.

The principal problem with video tapes is the lack of interactivity. The material is sequential and that's how you've got to access the material. This is perfectly acceptable if the course is rigid, but the majority of Master's degree programmes have an open structure to allow the student to access and spend time on those parts of the course they feel the need to work on.

Computer software

It's normally assumed that DL students on a Master's degree programme will possess or have access to a PC. The PC is quite invaluable when it comes to analysis and problem-solving and many DL schemes rely heavily on purpose-developed software as part of the programme. For example, the software application **Mathcad** is eminently suitable for modelling small-scale systems. By providing Mathcad files with embedded questions, the DL lecturer can set up a learning framework which requires active participation by the student, thereby allowing them to demonstrate their understanding of the problem.

Interactive CD-ROMs

A medium that is becoming increasingly popular in DL programmes is the CD-ROM (see Chapter 8).

If you are interested in pursuing a Master's DL course, ask the admissions tutor responsible for the programme if the course material is available on CD-ROM, and if not when will it be?

TACKLING ASSIGNMENTS

When on a Master's DL programme your progress will be monitored through the setting and marking of assignments. You should take these very seriously and ensure that you do not miss deadlines for submission. It's not uncommon for universities to dock marks from an assignment if it's submitted late. Plan your assignment carefully (see Chapter 2), remembering that there is no harm in submitting it early. This should be your general pattern anyway to avoid possible delays in the post. It's also good practice to obtain a certificate of posting (costing nothing) – in the event of it going astray in the Post Office system you will have some evidence of posting it. Always write your assignments using a wordprocessor and save them all on disc, so that if required, you can generate a copy with ease.

Marks and comments

Each assignment will be carefully marked and graded. Along with the grading, it's common practice for lecturers to add commentary and constructive criticism on each assignment. This is meant to act as feedback and gently correct any deficiencies that may be present in your assignment technique. You will notice that the specimen assignment front page (Figure 3 on page 31) has a large blank area for the lecturer's comments.

Self-help groups

Some universities strongly support the setting-up of self-help groups of its DL students, especially if several live close to each other. This type of interaction is useful, especially during the period when you are researching your main project and writing up your dissertation. This process can be significantly improved if you have access to electronic mail (**email**) via an Internet Service Provider (ISP). Using email is also a very convenient method of contacting the lecturing staff in your university.

Getting support

The problems of working in isolation can be quite exacting and you should not hesitate to discuss them with your supervisor – it's in his/her interest to see you succeed with the Master's programme. As mentioned above, you may be able to elicit financial help from your company in paying for the course. It's also worthwhile finding out whether there are other employees in the company that have an expertise in the subject area of your Master's degree programme. Drawing on several sources for information is a valuable means of learning.

FINAL THOUGHTS ON DL MASTER'S PROGRAMMES

These programmes require a special kind of commitment. If you're a family person, it's very important that you have the support of your spouse in this undertaking. Spending long periods locked away in your study on evenings and weekends requires some extra special understanding from other members of your family, especially your spouse. You may have to make sacrifices to earn this understanding.

CHECKLIST

- Make a realistic estimate of the time required for a DL Master's programme and ensure that you will have the time needed for the course. You will find information relating to expected commitment hours in the university's brochure.

- Find out whether your company is likely to cover the costs of the Master's programme and whether you can have additional time off for attending meetings at the university with your supervisor.

- Ensure that your PC is adequate for running the software that will be provided by the university. If it needs updating, estimate the costs and ask whether there are funds at your company for this purpose – part of the company's training programme.

CASE STUDIES

DL Master's degree in media communications
Ros works for a publishing house and is interested in a Master's Distance Learning programme on media communications.

Ros obviously works in an environment where deadlines are an everyday occurrence. This will have been good practice for her when she enrols on a Master's DL programme, as Ros will require self-discipline. Since Ros is doing a DL programme the distance from her chosen university is not a critical factor. There are a number of things that Ros could do:

- Find out which universities run Master's programmes in media communications. She needs to consult the *Careers Research and Advisory Centre (CRAC)* publication (see Chapter 1).

- Ros should also ask her line manager whether the company will cover the costs of the programme.

- She should find out whether her company will make a contribution towards the cost of a PC or its peripherals.

A DL Master's degree for becoming a headteacher
David has been teaching for five years and would like sometime in the future to aim for a headship in a state school. He is considering how a Master's degree in education would further his goal.

Skill updating amongst teachers and educationalists is regarded as an essential part of their profession. Changing teaching methods and the introduction of managerial methods into the profession has further emphasised the need for retraining. David, who is wishing to progress into a headship position, will invariably require a qualification beyond his first degree.

The nature of teaching in the state sector has changed over the past twenty years. Hitherto, emphasis had been placed on subject-based knowledge and acquiring teaching skills. Although still regarded as vitally important, teachers today are also expected to acquire skills relating to educational and financial management. This is especially true of teachers who are aiming for deputy headships or headships where a major part of their job specification will be to balance books and manage expenditure. This is particularly important for head-teachers of schools which have opted out of local education authority control.

In order for David to progress into a senior management position he should be looking at a suitable Distance Learning MA or M.Ed. programme which will probably have a module format.

Most Master's programmes in education will have a number of core modules and the remaining modules are selected from a wide choice, reflecting the student's personal interest. There will most probably be a dissertation to complete the course. Typically David should expect to see modules on:

- training and education in employment
- learning and assessment methods
- pupil development
- educational management
- leadership skills for educational environments
- special needs for science education
- special needs for technology education
- developing curricula material
- advances in language and literacy
- gender issues and education
- research methods for educational needs.

This list is by no means exhaustive but should indicate to David what modules to expect in a Master's programme. An attractive feature of a Master's programme in education is the flexibility to include modules that reflect contemporary thinking that is applicable to issues affecting current educational problems. This is certainly important in view of the changes that have taken place and are currently taking place in secondary and further education. David should also determine:

- whether his local education authority will pay for his university fees

- what remission time he can have to pursue the Master's programme.

DISCUSSION POINTS

1. Discuss with your spouse the problems that might arise if you embark on a DL programme, bearing in mind that a two-year course will require of you at least fourteen hours a week of private study.

2. Discuss your proposed DL Master's course with your employer and ascertain how it will enhance your promotional prospects in the company.

3. If possible, find someone else who has completed a DL Master's degree and discuss with them the difficulties they experienced.

8
Accessing Data and Information

Many Master's degree assignments and projects rely on the processing and interpretation of data. First of all the data must be accessed and stored in a suitable format which can be processed. This is where the PC comes into its own.

For many projects the data will already exist somewhere within a database. In fact a great deal of data does exist within databases and in many cases these can be accessed via a modem in your PC. Commercial databases hold a vast amount of information and details of how to access much of it is discussed in this chapter.

LOOKING AT DATA FROM OTHER INVESTIGATORS

Before you begin your project for your Master's degree you will have to decide which category it will fall in. In general there are two categories:

- Review and discuss the current state of a particular aspect of your chosen subject.

- Design and build a system or model to perform a specified set of functions followed by an investigation into its effectiveness.

Should you choose the first option your project will be in effect a review of the work already conducted by others who have researched and published material. If you are fortunate you may be able to offer a new contribution to knowledge or provide a new insight into the understanding of a particular phenomena. This, however, is not a requisite for attaining a Master's degree.

If you choose to design a system, whether it's mechanical, electrical, biological or based on a PC, you will probably, at some stage, require other people's data to make comparison with your own.

Data from written texts

Research is a cumulative process, as the knowledge that you discover will build upon what already exists. Therefore to perform an effective investigation you will need to be familiar with the contributions of other workers in the field. Normally this material can be found in the learned journals and textbooks devoted to your subject. Frequently the results of previous and current workers will be listed in tables or graphs in publications. You may even acquire data as ASCII files (text files that can be read directly into your PC).

There are a number of ways of converting printed tabular and graphical data into PC files. One of the most straightforward methods uses an image scanner interfaced to your PC, to create a computer image of the printed page. The image can then be subjected to **Optical Character Recognition** software to give you a text file that can be used in a wordprocessor.

Optical Character Recognition (OCR)

OCR software converts an image of a printed page into a usable PC file. It is customary to have a scanner linked up to a PC, and the PC will also have OCR software. During the installation of the scanner a software interface driver is sometimes installed as well. These drivers normally conform to the so-called TWAIN standard. When the OCR software is invoked it recognises the presence of the TWAIN driver and asks for the image source, either a file or a scanner.

When selecting a scanner the scanner window will appear which has a miniature area ready for the pre-scanned image. After the page is pre-scanned, the user is able to select (using drag and click with the mouse) the area of the printed text which they require converting. After scanning proper, the derived image is subjected to the OCR process. On completion the user is requested to save the data file.

Saving data

The data can be saved in a variety of file or wordprocessor formats. The data file will probably require some editing to remove the characters that the OCR failed to resolve. However, once that is done the data is available for further processing. If the original image has several text fields (a newspaper page, for example) it is sometimes necessary to partition the image into individual fields (**text zoning**). Once the OCR process starts, each zone will be converted in the order you set and the final document will have each zone as a separate paragraph. Some OCR software packages offer you the opportunity of verifying the document as it's being generated. This allows unrecognised words to be highlighted and corrected manually.

Commercial OCR software
There are a number of OCR software packages on the market and two well-known examples, which are very powerful and fast, are **TextBridge Pro** (Tel: (01734) 813230) and **Omnipage Pro** (Tel: (0171) 630 5586).

Extracting graphical data

Other researchers in your field may publish their data in graphical form. If you wish to use that data you can do so by creating [x,y] data from the 2D graphical image, which involves a **digitising** process. The task can be performed by using either a digitising tablet or preferably a software package such as **Ungraph**, available from **Biosoft** of Cambridge (Tel: (01223) 68622).

UnGraph can be used manually – you use the mouse to click on the plot points – or alternatively you can use the automatic line tracer which follows the plot trace and generates the [x,y] co-ordinates as it progresses (**Vectorising**). UnGraph has sufficient intelligence to correct for possible skew in the image and when in the automatic mode is mostly able to distinguish between the plot curve and the grid lines.

UnGraph needs a scanner
To make effective use of UnGraph you will require some means of obtaining an image of the graph that you wish to digitise, which normally requires the use of a scanner interfaced to your PC. The scanner must be able to produce line-art image files which is standard on all scanners. When UnGraph is invoked the user is provided with a menu bar of options. When selecting the Vectorising option the image appears on the screen (complete with skew) which can be corrected for by entering three co-ordinate positions.

In the **Auto Trace** mode the cursor will follow the plot line and generate digitised data points [x,y]. It will also remove the grid lines on the graph if necessary. In this mode extrapolation between the digitised points defaults to a linear algorithm. However, the user has the choice of a quadratic algorithm which is more appropriate for a sharply changing curve. Once the curve tracing is complete the user stores the data which can be accessed by other software applications.

Curve fitting

When confronted with a batch of data, you are justified in asking what to do with it now. In many applications (trend or economic forecasting) you would like to predict what happens outside the data batch you have. For example, you may have a graph showing wheat production in the UK between 1954 and 1996. Can you predict and how accurate will your prediction be for production for the rest of the decade? By using **regression** techniques (fitting a curve to a set of data points) you can gain a rough prediction of what will happen and you will also be able to attach a quantitative value on the quality of your prediction. This is a typical exercise that can be performed on a PC with relative ease.

Data access using a modem

An important medium through which information for research can be accessed is the Public Switch Network Service (PSNS – the telephone link). This is achieved by augmenting your PC with a modem (see Chapter 9). Once a modem is in place in your PC you will be able to access a variety of information sources. However, to access many of the most useful sources it will be necessary for your university or even you to subscribe to a number of **information vendors**. As in other markets, information is sold as a commodity. Most of the online information which is likely to be useful to the research student is hidden away in an array of databases.

Data from commercial databases

Users are charged to access and copy information from commercial databases. Databases are provided by many companies and organisations. Some databases can be accessed directly whereas others can only be accessed if you are a customer of an information wholesaler. In general an information retailer company will advertise the list of databases which its customers can access. It is therefore important to make the distinction between the database provider and the information retail company.

ACCESSING ONLINE SERVICES

In discussing the nature of databases, we shall look at their general classification. The significance of the databases with regard to specific academic disciplines can be determined accordingly. Some databases can be accessed directly whereas others require membership of an information retailing company. You will be able to determine from the university's computer centre which service providers are online.

JANET

The Joint Academic Network (JANET) is hosted on a mainframe at the Rutherford Appleton Laboratories in Oxfordshire. Its purpose is to facilitate academic information exchange not only nationally but also internationally. It is a resource that every new research student should investigate. The good news is that it is possible to access JANET with your own PC provided it is fitted with a modem. Many universities are connected to what is known as JIPS (JANET Internet Protocol Service) which gives direct access to many of the Internet services.

Commercial online services

There are several commercial sources which provide data for a large variety of fields. Much of this data is of a specialist nature. In general most of these companies permit its subscribers to access a range of databases. There are many tens of databases and you will find that several companies access the same ones. If the university is a subscriber it will pay an annual charge and an hourly rate as the services are used. In general it is possible to access the databases of one company by means of a **gateway** from another, a service that many online retailers offer. Many of these services are expensive but it is quite possible that your university subscribes to a number of them anyway. Many of these information retail companies also offer training sessions on their systems which ensures that the customers make efficient use of their services.

ESA-IRS

One of the major sources of scientific and engineering data is the **European Space Agency Information Retrieval Service** (ESA-IRS). It provides scientific, technical and aerospace information and has a powerful searching facility to seek out the required knowledge. The ESA-IRS databases contain millions of scientific and technical records which cover the broad scope of engineering knowledge. As the name suggests, ESA-IRS has particular strengths in the fields of aerospace, and its applications, including remote sensing, earth observation and microgravity. ESA-IRS does in fact have a vast number of technical databases which also contain relevant supporting information from distributed databases. It is extremely likely that your university will already have access to ESA-IRS through either the library resources or the university's computer centre. Alternatively ESA-IRS can be contacted on (0171) 323 7951.

Reuters

This is probably the most well-known company for providing global information services. Although it has gained an international reputation for comprehensive news coverage, it also supplies an information service to the world's financial institutions. Reuters has an array of databases (the 2000 series) which can be accessed for both financial information and news. Its product range features the following:

- *Financial market information*: real-time quotes from exchanges and over-the-counter market values.

- *Business information*: general information on companies and their performance.

- *Information management systems:* a suite of facilities which enables customers to analyse and efficiently access the Reuters financial data.

- *Transaction products*: information from foreign exchanges, futures, options and equities.

- *Media information*: international news gathered from Reuters' comprehensive network of news sources.

Reuters provides an attractive range of software products which run under Windows 95 on the PC (for example, **Business Briefing** and **Alert**) that enable a user to access their services. Reuters can be contacted on (0171) 250 1122.

Data-Star Dialog

This is one of the major contenders in the online information retail market which also incorporates the Swiss online company **RadioSuisse**. Dialog provides access to a substantial array of databases with particular specialisms in:

- science, technology and chemistry
- patents and intellectual property
- research and development information.

To add to the convenience of their searching methods for customers who require regular searches, Dialog provides an **Alert** service. As new data on a chosen subject becomes available, this information is relayed to the customer via email automatically. Dialog supplies an annual catalogue which features its database services, grouped as:

● *Business*: Business and Industry, International Directories and Company Finance, Product Information, US Directories and Company Finance.

● *News*: Newspaper Indexes, US Newspapers full text, Worldwide News.

● *Patents, Trademarks and Copyrights.*

● *Science*: Agrilculture and Nutrition, Chemistry, Computer Technology, Energy and Environment, Medicine and Biosciences, Pharmaceuticals, Technology and Engineering.

● *Social Sciences and Humanities.*

Each category has several databases attached to it and multiple searches can be performed on several databases at any one time. The *Dialog Database Catalogue 1997* gives a brief description of the contents of each database. Further information regarding Dialog's services can be obtained on (0171) 930 5503.

World Wide Web Sites

Over the past few years there has been an explosive growth of Web sites on the Internet. Some of these Web sites are sources of information that could be useful for students pursuing Master's degree programmes. The big problem is finding them. Since there are thousands of Web sites on the Internet you will need a suitable **browser** to access and interrogate them (see Chapter 9).

You will also need to go through an **Internet Service Provider** (ISP) such as CompuServe, AOL or Pipex. You will probably find that your university has access to the Internet. Again, make enquiries with the computer centre on what facilities the university has to offer.

Online service costs

Online services can be expensive so it will be in your and your university's interest to ensure that if you access these services you use them efficiently. If you are allocated a budget by your university for using online services make sure that you operate within the budget. Should you exceed your spending limit you may not be given a second chance.

REVIEWING DATA ON CD-ROMS

The CD-ROM has become a very important medium for information storage. Having evolved from the audio CD, over the past three years there has been a steady growth in the number of CD-ROM titles available on both sides of the Atlantic. They are also being used for archiving purposes in many institutions. There are several reasons for this widespread popularity.

- The manufacturing costs of CD-ROMs are now very low even for small batches (less than 50). There are many companies making CD-ROMs in the UK.

- Each CD-ROM can store in excess of 600 Mbyte of data. This data can be text, images, sound or video or even a combination of all types.

- With ever-improving data compression techniques it is likely that even more actual data will be stored on a standard CD-ROM.

- The data on a CD-ROM can be encrypted easily to prevent unauthorised access.

- CD-ROM drives are now standard on new PCs.

- As a storage medium the CD-ROM has a lifetime exceeding ten years.

- The data on CD-ROMs is permanent and cannot be erased or modified.

- CD-ROMs are also multi-session, which means that data can be added at a later time when it is available.

- The technology for manufacturing personal CD-ROMs is freely available costing less than £400.

- Options are available for integrating CD-ROM drives into **local area networks** (LANs) to make them a shared resource. For example, **Netware Loadable Modules** (NLMs) exist for this function.

It is therefore hardly surprising that there has been a great deal of attention shown in the CD-ROM. For the research student the CD-ROM is also an important source of information. Although there are many CD-ROMs which have multimedia data on, most of it will not have any value as research material. However, many institutions are using CD-ROMs for archiving and cataloguing; for example, libraries, museums and actuaries. In fact much of the information held by **Her Majesty's Stationery Office** (HMSO) is available on CD-ROM (Tel: (01603) 695498). One of the most comprehensive sources of currently available CD-ROMs is *CD-ROMs in Print 1997* (CD-ROM version) from **Meckler**. An alternative source is Microinfo (Tel: (01420) 86848).

Commercial CD-ROM suppliers

There are several companies that sell information on CD-ROMs and this information covers virtually all aspects of knowledge. Because of the very fluid nature of information, current data will be out of date tomorrow. An updating system is therefore required and it is customary for a client to become an annual subscriber to a company selling information as databases on CD-ROMs. This means that every two months or every quarter they will be supplied with a new set of CD-ROMs with the new information on to supersede the old ones. One well-known service is **Whitackers** CD-ROM of *Books in Print*.

Newspapers

A number of national newspapers and magazines are also available on CD-ROM, including:

- *The Guardian*
- *The Times* and *The Sunday Times*
- *Changing Times*
- *The Economist*
- *Financial Times*
- *The Independent*
- *The Telegraph*
- *Il Sole 24 Ore* (Italian)
- *AFP-DOC* (French)
- *AFP Sciences* (French).

The above titles are available from **Chadwyck-Healey** (Tel: (01223) 215512). They are updated on a regular basis.

CHECKLIST

- If you are likely to access the Internet on a regular basis check with your supervisor to see if you can use the facilities in the university.

- Ask one of the librarians in your university library for a list of all the CD-ROM titles they possess. They will probably be available for access only and not to take away.

- If you are buying a new PC check for special deals on modems and ask around for the best.

CASE STUDIES

A Master's degree involving the analysis of geographical information

Lynda has registered on an M.Sc. programme in social economics and needs information for her dissertation on geographical economic trends in British society.

This type of information is available in various formats. Lynda should be looking at a **Geographical Information Service** (GIS). A GIS is in effect a digitised map which turns statistical and geographic data into meaningful information for analysis purposes. In order for a GIS to be effective it is normally compatible with a well-known database format such as **Lotus 1-2-3** or **Microsoft Excel**. Lynda will discover that a quality GIS will have multiple **what if** and **show me where** scenarios to allow the results of her analysis to be compared. Lynda will be able to combine map features such as points, lines or areas, or create buffers around several map features and automatically aggregate the data. By applying statistical tools Lynda will be able to derive economic trends according to geographical location. Typically Lynda should be looking at a suitable database and a PC-based GIS, for example:

- CD-ROM database available from HMSO, *25 Years of Social Trends.*

- Atlas GIS available from Adept Scientific, Letchworth (Tel: (01462) 480055).

Selecting a dissertation project that reflects an individual's needs

Tony has been accepted on a Master's programme on multimedia technology. For his dissertation project, Tony is planning the design of an educational tool that accesses and uses the Internet as a teaching resource.

This is an interesting project as the Internet has become a powerful agent for disseminating information. Tony will be faced with a number of problems:

- The amount of information on the Internet is so vast, he must devise a criterion procedure for sifting through it.

- Much of the material on Web sites has a hypertext structure (derived from **hypertext make-up language** – HTML) where referenced words lead to other pages.

- He will need to learn about a suitable design method for automatically accessing Web sites which fall within his criterion envelope.

To develop an educational tool for interrogating various Internet sites, that has a well-defined envelope, Tony should be looking seriously at the JAVA programming language that has been designed specifically for Internet applications (for example, Visual J++ from Microsoft, Tel: (0345) 002000). If Tony is not familiar with programming techniques, he must ensure that he takes the option of module(s) on his Master's programme that provide these.

DISCUSSION POINTS

1. If you are considering using data from other sources, discuss with your supervisor what software packages are the most appropriate.

2. Discuss with the manager in the computer centre what databases are available on CD-ROM and from online services. Since it's likely that the library will also stock databases on CD-ROM, it is worthwhile having similar discussions with the appropriate librarian.

9
Using a PC in your Master's Programme

An indispensable tool for all students these days is the personal computer (PC). The remarkable advances made in the USA in microelectronics over the past fifteen years has resulted in the availability of low-cost, high-performance PCs.

If you do not possess a PC, you should seriously consider buying one in the near future. As an easy guide and introduction to PCs, their technology and their peripherals (the things you can add to a PC to enhance its functionality), the reader is recommended to the author's *Buying a Personal Computer* (see Further Reading).

Whatever subject you choose for your Master's programme, you will invariably find a PC a very useful asset. In fact, it is essential that you have access to a PC hosting suitable wordprocessor software for the production of your dissertation or thesis.

WHAT TO LOOK FOR IN A PC

PCs these days are quite complex pieces of equipment and come with a wide range of options. Typically a PC will comprise:

- a system enclosure (main box)
- a colour monitor (screen)
- a keyboard
- a mouse
- stereo speakers.

The system enclosure may be designed to reside either on the desk-top (with the monitor on top of it) or as a tower, the latter being preferable since it can be tucked away under the desk. In the system enclosure you will find the majority of the electronic components and these are attached to a printed circuit board known as the **Motherboard**.

Central Processing Unit

At the heart of every PC you will find what is known as the Central Processing Unit (CPU) which executes the **intelligence** of the PC. If you are buying a new PC, it will most probably be based on the **Intel Pentium Processor**. However, if your needs are for wordprocessing only, a PC based on the earlier Intel 486 processor is more than adequate for your needs.

The **speed** of the CPU is determined by what is known as the clock speed which is measured in millions of cycles per seconds (MHz – megahertz). Typically modern PCs with a Pentium Processor will have clock speeds ranging from 90 MHz to 200 MHz. Generally the higher the clock speed the faster the PC and the more expensive it is.

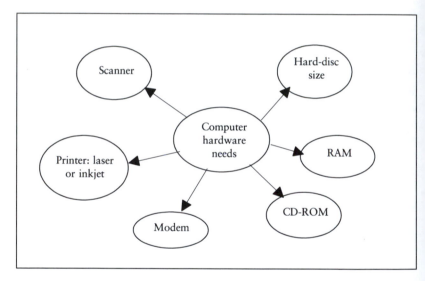

Fig. 5. Overview of PC hardware needs.

RAM

The Pentium Processor executes programs (series of instructions) which reside in the system memory known as RAM (Random Access Memory). This is measured in millions of bytes (Mbyte). Most PCs are supplied with a standard 8 Mbyte but this can be easily increased to 16 or 32 Mbyte with relatively little cost. If you have an application that manipulates large amounts of data (images, for example) the more RAM you have the faster the PC will operate.

Hard-disc

The hard-disc unit is where programs and data are stored on the PC. The **storage capacity** of these units can range from 850 Mbyte to 5 Gbyte (Giga – 1,000 Mega) and more. It is commonplace to find new PCs furnished with 1.2 Gbyte as standard. It's not only the storage capacity that's important but also the **access time** (average time it takes to transfer data to and from the hard-disc), but this only becomes significant when the PC is used for special applications. Normally the access time is less than 12 msec (milli-seconds = 0.001 seconds).

CD-ROM drive

Every PC bought today will have a CD-ROM drive which is for reading programs and data stored on CD-ROMs. A CD-ROM can hold about 650 Mbyte of data and the performance of a CD-ROM drive is measured by its speed which relates to the **data transfer speed**. These days this is Six Speed, Eight Speed or even Ten Speed. The original speed was 150 kbyte per second. A Six Speed is therefore 6 x 150 or 900 kbyte per second.

DVD

Some CD-ROM drives are of the new design, **Digital Versatile Disc** (DVD), where the discs have a capacity of about 4.7 Gbyte for a single layer. DVD-ROMs may have single layer, double layer and even double-sided layers. With two layers per side this would give a total storage capacity of 18.8 Gbyte per disc which is quite sufficient for holding a full-length feature video. Using the MPEG-2 compression standard, 4.7 Gbyte can store 135 minutes of video data.

Graphics

Inside the main unit there is a circuit board (**graphics card**) for driving the monitor and producing the image on the screen. Most applications only require static images with a good range of colours (colour depth). When considering graphics you will often come across the word **resolution** which refers to the number of active dots on the screen. For a 15-inch monitor you should have it set to a minimum of 800 x 600 screen dots. This provides reasonable resolution. If, on the other hand, you have a 17-inch monitor you should be looking for a minimum of 1,024 x 760 dots with 4 Mbyte of graphics memory.

Video on the PC

There is lot of emphasis these days on how well PCs are able to play video from CD-ROMs (multimedia PCs). If you are likely to require this from your PC you should ensure that the graphics card is **MPEG compatible** (a standard set up by the **Moving Picture Expert Group**).

Animation
If you are likely to have a need to use a lot of animation you should be thinking carefully about using a **3D graphics card** which has special features for displaying perspective graphics.

Sound
It is customary these days for every PC to host a **sound card** that has a range of functions. The stereo speakers supplied with the PC are connected directly to the sound card. Alternatively the output from the sound card can be connected to a hi-fi system. Typically the functions of the sound card include:

● sound generation
● text to speech
● sound and speech recording
● speech recognition (with the appropriate software)
● musical sound generation.

There is also a connector on the sound card to allow a MIDI instrument to be linked to your PC. The same connector is also used as a games port to support a joy-stick. Many CD-ROMs have short video files with attached sound tracks (known as .AVI files – audio video interlaced) which can be played with simultaneous sound and video.

LOOKING AT PERIPHERALS FOR YOUR PC

It is common practice these days to attach peripherals to PCs in order to enhance their functionality. There are three means by which peripherals are interfaced to a PC.

● using an expansion card
● using a serial port
● using the parallel port.

Expansion cards
On the motherboard, in the main unit, there is a row of **expansion connectors** (slots) which accommodate what are known as **expansion**

cards. Some peripherals, such as image scanners, come with their own expansion card which you are expected to insert into an expansion connector on the motherboard. If you have an occasion to open up the main unit you will find that the graphics card occupies one of the expansion slots.

Serial port

On the back of the PC's unit you will find two connectors with pins (either 25 or 9 pins). These are the **serial ports** and several peripherals are connected to the PC via a serial port. You will probably find that the mouse occupies one, leaving one free. Typically the peripherals that would use a serial port are:

- an external modem
- a graphics tablet – to allow free hand drawing
- some printers.

Data transmission through the serial port can sometimes be quite slow since it only has one transmission channel for the data to travel along.

Parallel port

All PCs have at least one parallel port which is used almost exclusively for attaching a **printer** to your PC. The parallel port is always a 25-way socket with holes as opposed to pins. When you buy a printer it should be supplied with a cable which connects directly in the parallel port with a **Centronics** plug on the other end which connects to the printer.

Printers

This is an essential peripheral for every PC. During your time of study for your Master's degree you will rely quite heavily upon the printer. Handwritten material is not normally acceptable these days and written assignments are expected to be produced on a wordprocessor. The printers available today can produce very high quality output, even images embedded in text made up of a variety of different font sizes and designs. And the good news if that their cost is surprisingly low considering the technology involved in their designs. There are two features to look for in the performance of a printer:

- *Resolution* – should be a minimum of 300 dots per inch (dpi) or even better 600 dpi.

- *Print speed* – should be a minimum of 6 pages per minute (ppm).

The first low-cost printer was the **matrix printer,** with a print head comprising an array of pins which were ejected forward onto a ribbon to make a character impression. They are still made but they are up against some stiff competition from other more versatile designs.

Laser printers
These days **monochrome** (black) laser printers are available for only a few hundred pounds and they represent very good value for money. They are capable of reproducing monochrome images with good contrast (several shades of grey). Every laser printer has a toner cartridge which is capable of printing several thousand pages of A4 paper, and although they are expensive to replace they do last for a very long time.

You will find that many laser printers come with two interface connectors. If this is the case you can use either the serial or the parallel link. The more expensive laser printers will come with a third option to enable it to be attached to a network of computers.

Although colour laser printers are available they tend to be quite expensive (£2,000+), but you may be fortunate in having one available in the university's computer centre.

Inkjet and bubblejet printers
The alternative cheaper design to the laser printer is one based on the inkjet or bubble jet technology. The technology of inkjet printers has come on enormously over the past few years and the print quality is very high. Resolutions in excess of 300 dpi are commonplace. However, the print rate is still rather slow, much less than laser printers. The printer head has an array of very small nozzles and minute droplets of ink are squirted onto the paper to form the character or image.

Some inkjet printers can offer very high resolution (720 dpi), although the print rate tends to be very slow. The ink for these devices is contained in cartridges. You will only get a few thousand pages printed for each refull. They tend to be quite expensive and they have a use-by date once they have been opened.

Colour printers
If you require a low-cost colour printer there are several inkjet models available which give surprisingly good results. With advancement in

technology the quality of output from inkjet printers has progressed accordingly. Resolutions of 720 dpi are not unusual. It's quite possible that you may requite colour illustrations for your dissertation in which case a colour inkjet printer is well worth considering since they are available for only a few hundred pounds.

Ink colours

Good quality colour inkjet printers require four coloured inks (**cyan, magenta, yellow,** and **black – CMYK**) and it is usual to have the CMY inks in a separate cartridge to the black. Although the printers themselves are quite low cost their maintenance is not. The ink cartridges are expensive and they don't last very long. This, of course, depends on the intensity of your colour printing.

Printers and Windows 95

Each printer you connect to your PC will require a **printer driver** (a software utility) which is usually supplied with the printer. Once you connect the printer to your PC and turn it on, if you are using Windows 95, it will recognise that a newperipheral is attached. It will then lead you through the installation procedure for the printer driver – it should be quite a painless process.

FAX/modem

Another peripheral which has now become essential is a FAX/modem which enables the PC to communicate with other systems via the telephone link (also known as the **Public Switched Telephone Network – PSTN**). The FAX/modem serves a dual purpose, as both a FAX machine and a communication unit. They are available as either an external unit or an internal expansion card which is accommodated in the PC – the internal design is normally cheaper.

When buying a FAX/modem you should ensure that it conforms to at least the **V.34 standard**. Data transfer rates are measured in baud and a V.34 modem will operate at 28,880 bits per second (bps). However, there are new modems on the market that will operate at twice this figure, 57,760 bps. This will ensure maximum data transfer rate on the PSTN.

FAX software

When you buy a FAX/modem the software that comes with it will enable you to use your PC as a FAX machine. In fact within Windows 95 there is a FAX software utility. With it you will be able to receive and transmit FAXs.

Typically, the FAX software offers you another printer option but instead of printing your document it is FAXed off. For example, you may have written a document on your PC using a wordprocessor. By selecting Printer Set-up from the menu you have the option of making the FAX/modem the active printer. When you choose to print the document you are prompted for a telephone FAX number. Once entered the document is sent.

Using the modem for data access

Once a FAX/modem is in place in your PC you will be able to access a variety of information sources, either through Bulletin Boards or through the Internet and the World Wide Web (WWW – or just WEB). However, to access many of the most useful sources it will be necessary for your university or even you to subscribe to an information vendor (see Chapter 8).

Browsers

There are thousands of Web sites available for visiting all over the world but most of them are in the USA. To perform an effective visit you will need a software utility known as a **browser**. There are several available including **Explorer** from **Microsoft** and **Navigator** from **Netscape**. The latter is augmented by third party utilities known as **plug-ins** which enable you to access the features embedded in data files on offer at Web sites. Remember data files are not only text, but also sound, image, video or 3D animation.

Image scanners

A further peripheral that will enhance the functionality of your PC is the image scanner. As with the other peripherals, the price of scanners has fallen dramatically over the past few years – a good quality scanner will cost less than £400. Three designs are available: flat-bed, page-feed and hand-held, although the most versatile is the flat-bed design. Normally a scanner will come with its own expansion card that you are expected to insert into an expansion slot in the PC's main unit. The performance of a scanner will depend on the following characteristics:

- *Colour depth* – minimum 24-bit true colour
- *Resolution* – minimum 300 dots per inch (dpi).

Whatever the colours of the picture you are scanning, they should be preserved in the digitised image that appears on the screen.

Images and memory
You will find that colour images take up an enormous amount of memory. The more RAM you have in your PC the faster the processing rates. If you have to deal with a lot of colour images, 32 Mbytes may be a suitable amount of RAM to have installed in your PC.

Image formats for storage
There are a huge number of image formats used to save images on disc, indicated by the file name tag. The most common ones are:

- Tagged Image File Format (.TIF)
- Microsoft's Bit Mapped (.BMP)
- Encapsulated Post Script (.EPS)
- Microsoft Paintbrush (.PCX)
- Joint Photographic Experts Group (.JPG).

When saving images on disc they are usually compressed in order to save disc space. One frequently used compression method is based on the **Lempel-Ziv algorithm**.

Applications of image scanners
For a student on a Master's degree programme, the image scanner can have several applications. However, these will be dependent upon the software utilities on the host PC.

Scanning pictures or figures for your dissertation
When writing your dissertation you may need diagrams or pictures and some of these can be scanned directly into your wordprocessor using the image scanner. Provided acknowledgement is given, normally you do not have to worry about the copyright issue. If you decide to publish your dissertation at a later date you have to be cautious of any breach of copyright.

Converting page-text into a wordprocessor document
You may very well want to import text from another source, especially if you are using long quotations. An image scanner linked to your PC hosting **Optical Character Recognition** (OCR) software will perform this task. Once pages have been scanned in using the **line-art** format the OCR will convert it into a text file which can be loaded directly into your wordprocessor.

Taking a photograph of a thin object
Surprisingly, an image scanner can be used very effectively for taking
photographs of thin objects such as a CD label or a leaf. This can
only be done with thin objects since the focusing depth of the scanner
is only a few millimetres – experiment and see what results you can
get. It is much cheaper and quicker than using traditional photographic methods.

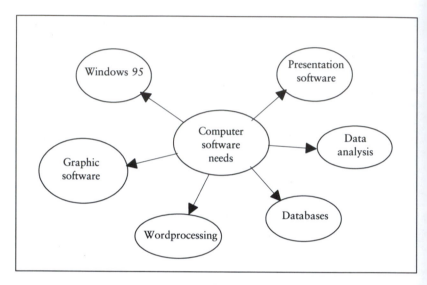

Fig. 6. Overview of PC software needs.

Other peripherals
For an introduction to the wide range of other peripherals, including
video capture, digital photographs and sound recording, see the
author's *Buying a Personal Computer* (How To Books 1996).

REVIEWING SOFTWARE FOR YOUR PC

Hardware is only half the story. To make effective use of your PC
you will also need good software (see Figure 6). The type of software
you will require for your Master's will depend upon the nature of
the subject you are researching. Engineering and science have a wealth
of software applications packages whereas the Humanities are more
limited, although there are several Concordance software packages
available for performing literature word count and word frequency

analysis. As a postgraduate student you will be entitled to some very generous discounts. Make enquiries in the students union and also in the university's computer centre to see what's on offer.

Windows 95

When buying a new PC it is customary to have Windows 95 from Microsoft pre-installed. Although it's not the only operating system for the PC (the environment in which programs run), it has received the greatest amount of support through the release of new PC software designed to run under Windows 95. Within Windows 95 you can have any number of applications active at any one time (depending on the amount of RAM you have in your PC).

There are various methods for exchanging data between the active software programs and one of the easiest methods is to use the clipboard. You copy something to the clipboard in one application, move to the new application and paste the data from the clipboard into the application. Generally speaking, Windows 95 runs most effectively on a Pentium PC furnished with a minimum of 16 Mbyte of RAM.

Integrated software suites

Whatever your chosen subject it's highly likely that you will need to use the standard PC software packages, namely a wordprocessor, a spreadsheet, a scheduler and a database. These are so universal that they tend to be combined into what is known as integrated software suites. Several commercial products are available; for example, **Office** and **Works,** both from **Microsoft, WordPerfect Suite** from **Corel** and **SmartSuite** from **Lotus.** Some of these are available with an educational discount. For a general PC user an integrated software suite (ISS) is usually a good option. In fact many PC suppliers bundle an ISS with their machine.

Commercial example – Lotus SmartSuite
To give an example of what to expect in an ISS we shall have a closer look at SmartSuite from Lotus. This package comprises five components; a key design feature of ISSs is the mechanism whereby data or information can be exchanged between each component with total ease. For example, if you are running the wordprocessor and the spreadsheet at the same time, you can transfer a block of cells from the spreadsheet directly to the wordprocessor still retaining the cell format. The five components of SmartSuite are:

- *Word Pro*: a fully comprehensive wordprocessing package with dictionary, thesaurus and grammar checker. Facilities for drawing, producing tables and charts and generating mathematical equations.

- *1-2-3*: an extensive spreadsheet which comes with pre-defined templates called Smartmasters. The usual in-cell editing with a vast number of processes of manipulating arrays of numbers.

- *Freelance*: a presentation package which enables the design and construction of material for overhead presentations. Several templates are provided with lots of clip-art figures. A necessary feature for your dissertation presentation.

- *Approach*: an easy-to-use database with several ready-made templates to help you along the learning curve of creating useful databases.

- *Organiser*: somewhat similar to the manual version with daily diary for lecture schedules, tutorials, revision planning and general working out of assignments schedules. Also useful for notes, addresses and telephone numbers.

This should serve to give you an indication of what to expect from an ISS.

One other thing to bear in mind is the amount of **hard-disc space** that an ISS will take. Smartsuite 96 takes up 150 Mbyte.

When you purchase a legitimate version of the software you will also get a full set of **manuals** which are quite invaluable as you rise up the learning curve of the product.

Modelling software

It is quite possible that your Master's degree programme will involve a certain amount of statistics and mathematical modelling. This is true for so many programmes that a high level of mathematical skill is expected as a matter of course. The PC can be of great benefit for this since it is able to process and display vast amounts of data. The highly visual aspect of the PC with its high resolution graphics makes it a very useful tool in visualising models and performing simulations.

Commercial modelling software – Mathcad
There are several statistical software packages available, although

many of the more comprehensive ones tend to be quite expensive even with educational discounts. For many modelling applications, **Mathcad** from **Adept Scientific** (Tel: (01462) 480055) is more than adequate. Mathcad can be used to tackle a whole range of problems and uses a direct schematic input. It deals with tables, graphs, equations, matrices and analytical expressions. It's ideal for solving differential equations (both linear and non-linear) and even performs animations of solutions.

To add to its appeal there are numerous **Function Packs** which specialise in specific applications, such as statistics, economics, electronics engineering. Mathcad has several pre-defined statistical operations which can be invoked with ease. Data can be imported into Mathcad from disc files or manually through the keyboard.

Precautions

There are a few measures that you will be well advised to adopt during your Master's programme. The first is to keep back-ups of all your work on floppy discs. Although hard-disc integrity is better today than it ever has been, they still go wrong. The need to keep back-ups is especially urgent if your PC is a lap-top design. These are very vulnerable to theft, sadly even in universities, and it only takes one careless moment.

CHECKLIST

- If you are buying a new PC look through a number of PC magazines and list the various specifications used to classify each machine.

- Determine which software packages you will be using on your Master's programme. Ask the module lecturers for details. Enquire at the university's computer centre whether the software is available at a reasonable student discount.

- Microsoft (Tel: (0345) 002000) and Borland (Tel: (0990) 561281) sometimes run student discounted versions of their software packages. Make enquiries with both companies to see if any of their products are of interest to you.

- If you are using an ISS try to identify where each of its components will be useful in your Master's programme and make sure that you are sufficiently familiar with it in order to maximise its potential.

CASE STUDIES

Using a PC to access data from CD-ROMs

John is studying for an M.Sc. in human geography and is interested in social geographical trends which he hopes to make the theme of his dissertation.

Much of the information that John is after can be found on *The 1991 Census on CD-ROM* (available from **Chadwyck-Healey** at Cambridge, Tel: (01223) 215512). This is a single integrated package that combines the statistics with mapping at all geographic levels. It has facilities specifically for the analysis and presentation of census material. It also includes **Vector Boundary Mapping** which can be used for enumerating district and all higher levels. John will be able to produce tables, graphs and maps, on the same screen, and combine census variables to create new statistics and mapping information. John should:

● Find out whether the census CD-ROM is available in his department, the library or computer centre.

● Ascertain whether he is able to borrow the CD-ROM and for how long.

● Ensure that his PC has at least a quad speed CD-ROM drive, 8 Mbyte of RAM and SVGA graphics.

● Ensure he has a quality printer to reproduce his maps, tables and graphs – he should therefore be considering a colour inkjet printer.

Specifying a PC in a humanities Master's programme

Dorothy is thinking about buying a PC to help her with the Master's programme that she has just started on cultural politics.

Dorothy has been informed that the software used during the course is already available on the PCs in the university's computer centre but it would be helpful to her if she had a database on her PC. Since she will have several assignments over the duration of the programme, she will need a wordprocessor and in view of the suggestion regarding the database it would be appropriate for Dorothy to invest in a suitable ISS. Before she does this she should:

- Ascertain what databases are compatible with the software that she will be using in the computer centre. Dorothy needs to know this as it's likely that she'll want to transfer data from the work she performs on the university's computers to her own using a floppy disc.

- Find out whether the university operates a student discount scheme on the ISS.

Specifying a PC for use in a Master's in biology

Tony has registered on a Master's programme degree in environmental biology. He has opted to do the modules that involve a significant amount of ecological system modelling. He is thinking about what PC to buy and appropriate software.

Although the university will make available all the software tools that Tony needs for his Master's, it will probably be in his interest to buy a software package which can be used for modelling systems constructed from differential equations. Tony should be:

- Thinking about a Pentium PC with: 16 Mbyte of RAM, 1.2 Gbyte hard-disc, 6 speed CD-ROM and integrated software suite.

- Finding out about modelling software such as Mathcad or VisSim (available from Adept Scientific, Tel: (01462) 480055), both of which provide graphical outputs.

- Determining whether the PC hardware and the modelling software are available with a student discount.

DISCUSSION POINTS

- A PC will probably represent a significant investment for a student on a Master's degree programme. Taking your own study needs and financial resources into account, make a list of the pros and cons of buying a PC (or upgrading your existing system).

● If you have decided to buy a new PC, discuss the various options available for obtaining finance for it. Several mail order companies offer very attractive deals – look through a few PC magazines.

● Discuss your needs as far as peripherals are concerned. You will definitely need a printer, but which design? Think about the other peripherals cited in this chapter.

10
Planning Your Project and Writing Your Dissertation

The final task in your research programme is to write up your thesis or dissertation, but the form of that final written work will depend on decisions taken earlier in relation to the nature and scope of the project.

THE NATURE OF THE PROJECT

Generally speaking, the work you perform for your dissertation or thesis project should be of an investigative nature. This requires more than just discussion of a particular topic – you should aim to investigate an issue in an analytical manner. Much of your investigation will be spent in considering what other people have contributed to the theme of your project. After all, you will be basing your contribution upon the work of others. This applies whether you are advancing a new theory or investigating the current understanding of a particular subject.

In general there are two approaches to a Master's dissertation or thesis.

- *The first approach* is a survey of current knowledge relating to the theme of your project. You will be expected to advance arguments of how your theme falls within the context of what has been investigated previously. You will therefore be investigating what other people have done and reviewing the significance of their contribution.

- *The second approach* involves the investigation of an actual experiment designed and executed by you. This may necessitate the construction of an experimental model, which enables testing, from which a further understanding of your project theme can be gleaned.

The former, reviewing current understanding, is more applicable to a dissertation of a taught Master's programme whereas the latter, designing and building a model, is applicable to a research Master's. However, this is not a hard and fast rule.

CONSIDERING THE DISSERTATION FOR A TAUGHT MASTER'S

A major part of your taught Master's degree programme is the project for your dissertation. A dissertation project may take one of the following forms, depending on the subject matter:

- A **thorough review** of a particular aspect relating to the course material – how various writers have considered your chosen topic, including a historical perspective and a review of progress made since starting, to the present day.

- An **analysis or investigation** into an aspect relating to your course subject and how it affects or influences developments in other areas of your subject.

- A **genuine contribution to new knowledge** – usually difficult at this level except for a Life Science Master's programme.

- A **design of a new product, device or strategy** which will find an application in an industrial or commercial organisation.

It is quite normal for the student to suggest an idea for a project. Alternatively the student's tutor or supervisor will have a stock of possible projects. Either way the student will be expected, at some stage, to submit a **written proposal**, comprising:

- possible title

- main objective of the project – why you think it's worth doing and an assessment of its value as an academic exercise and in a broader context

- resources needed

- a break-down of the project into constituent parts

- timescale for carrying out the investigation and completing the project.

Your supervisor will be convinced or otherwise on the strength of your proposal and whether it's viable. The result will be acceptance, modification or rejection.

Acceptance
When your supervisor accepts your project proposal, this usually indicates that he/she has confidence in your idea and more importantly in you as an individual to conduct the work needed to see it through to a satisfactory conclusion.

Acceptance with modification
It's quite possible that your supervisor finds merit in your proposal but feels that it's too ambitious, or fails to define its focus accurately enough or should be broadened to include important aspects that you have neglected. When this happens, you will be offered guidance to get the balance right. This guidance is part of the learning process and is valuable. It should not be regarded as personal criticism.

Rejection
This is only likely to happen if the theme of your project proposal is trivial or not worth investigating. When this happens it usually indicates that you haven't given sufficient thought and effort to preparing your project proposal. You will invariably be given an opportunity to rework your proposal after you have received further guidance from your supervisor.

Role of your supervisor
It's quite common for candidates to rely on their supervisor to provide a project for their Master's dissertation. However, your understanding of what is required should be made clear in the project proposal that you will have to prepare for your supervisor. Make sure, during your preliminary discussion with your supervisor, that you gain as clear an understanding as you can of the expectations. Do not be afraid to ask questions, however trivial they may seem.

During the time allocated to the project work it is very important that you maintain close links with your supervisor to ensure that you are on the right track and the standard of your work is acceptable. In many instances a supervisor will only see you periodically and assume that you are getting on with the work. It's a deliberate policy not to over-supervise a Master's degree project unless it's running into severe problems. The golden rule relating to supervision is:

> **Keep your supervisor informed of what you are doing.**

Surveying material for your dissertation

As mentioned above, there are at least two approaches to tackling a Master's degree dissertation project. The first method will involve reviewing, surveying and possibly investigating the theme of your project. You will be required to review appropriate references relating to the current state of knowledge of your project theme. Your supervisor should be able to point you in the right direction for this task, but don't forget to use the resources in the university library (see Chapter 5).

When you are surveying the state of knowledge, you must be careful not to neglect any important aspect or contribution. Should you do this, your survey will be considered incomplete and you may be asked to revise it. Keep in touch with your supervisor and ask them for their opinion.

THESIS FOR A RESEARCH M.PHIL.

When researching for an M.Phil. degree you will be expected to investigate a thesis project. Sometimes it may be appropriate to tackle this investigation in the same way as suggested for a dissertation – in essence a survey type of project. However, in many instances, you will be expected to apply the research tools and methods passed on to you by your supervisor. This type of investigation may involve:

- reviewing the current literature
- methodology and designing a model
- designing an experiment or a series of experiments
- collecting data
- analysis of data.

Each stage must be carefully planned and scheduled accordingly. Time management is crucial since you have a limited amount of time to complete the investigation and write it up in a thesis.

Collecting data

You may find yourself in the fortunate position of being able to use other people's data and apply your own analysis to it. The data may be available in tabulated or graphical form and it will be up to you to translate it into usable data files for your PC.

Many research projects, however, involve the collection of raw data – if this is the case a lot of your time will be spent doing just that. Before this process can begin, a great deal of careful thought is needed. Firstly, you must establish exactly what you are trying to measure – you should be involving your supervisor in this aspect of the research. Once you have determined what information you require, you must ask whether this is sufficient to test what you are investigating.

Planning a questionnaire

In many applications you cannot afford to make mistakes because you'll only have one shot at it. For instance, if you require knowledge of what people think of XYZ then you may have to generate your own questionnaire and conduct a poll. The wording of the questionnaire is crucial. It will be difficult and very time-consuming for you to repeat the exercise with an amended version. The design of the questionnaire is therefore critical and requires a lot of thought in order to get it right. The questionnaire will be your **measuring system** and the quality of the information you derive from it will be in part dependent on the quality of its design. Try and ascertain exactly what information you require in order to test what you are investigating. Make every effort to avoid ambiguous questions and use plain English.

Multifaceted problems and the general system model

You will probably find that the subject you are investigating is **multifaceted** – a problem with several variables. Consider the abstract case where there are several influencing factors (inputs) on a system and you are trying to investigate the response of the system to them (see Figure 7). This can be regarded as the **general system model**. The responses come in the form of observations which can be made of the system.

Your thesis project may only be concerned with one input and one observation. But the system could be an unknown entity (the most likely case) where all the influencing factors affect each of the observations. Any one of the observations could be a *weighted* response of all the inputs. To make matters worse, the responses could be non-linear – no easy mathematical relationship relating them,

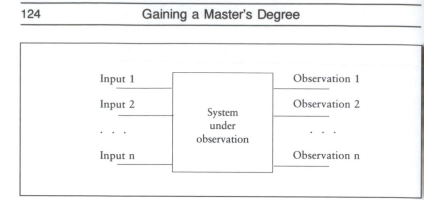

Fig. 7. Schematic representation of multifaceted system.

although there might be interdependence between them. It's possible that previous investigators may have established links between some of the inputs and some of the observations. This information can be used to guide your thinking on the problem and how you are going to investigate it.

Example of a system

Let's consider a real example of this abstract model: the **incidence of young offenders**. The **system** is the body of young offenders and possible **inputs** to the system are:

- exposure to violence on television
- free availability of video nasties
- breakdown in discipline in the home
- failure in the education system
- racial tension
- peer pressure
- availability of soft and hard drugs.

It's quite possible that some additional inputs are not included because their influence has been underestimated or simply overlooked.

The **observations** of the young offenders system will come in terms of statistics relating to their behaviour and these could be:

- severity of crime with age
- number of police cautions per offender
- number which come from broken homes
- number from an ethnic or other minority background

- number which come from socially deprived areas
- number of under-achievers in school.

In the ideal world (the perfect experiment) you would like to vary only one input and remove all the others (or at least keep them constant) and look at the responses (observations). This is almost impossible, but it doesn't stop researchers from trying to investigate the problem.

Part of the investigation would be an attempt to model the system using a mathematical framework, or just to analyse the statistics to determine a causal correlation. You may even attempt to attach an empirical weighting to each of the inputs in order to determine the significance and sensitivity of each one. This may be accomplished as a result of your analysis. You will find that as a researcher this general framework model is applicable to a whole range of issues.

Establishing links

As a new researcher you may be tempted to try and establish a whole range of links between influences and observations. This mistake is often made – biting off more than you can chew – but the condition is usually rectified with experience as the project progresses. There are two primary reasons for this condition to arise:

1. Your initial proposal wasn't defined tightly enough which may indicate that insufficient thought had been put into it. This could be because of your lack of understanding of the problem, which is not uncommon and should not be regarded as criticism but part of the learning process.

2. You were far too ambitious in what you thought could be achieved in the time; this is invariably a result of inexperience in research and again should be considered as part of the learning process.

It is usually very difficult to avoid either or both of these scenarios, but what is of importance is how they are resolved. This will be a true test of merit.

Analysis

Analysis is only possible when you have some data to analyse. During the planning stages of your research you should have determined what you were intending to investigate and set a series of **measurements** to yield the data you require. The word 'measurements' is used in the broadest sense of the word. In many instances it could simply refer to information which you have searched for.

In the general model discussed above, we had inputs and observations and in your analysis you will attempt to establish some connection, link, correlation or pattern between them. By achieving this you will be in a position to characterise the system (or problem) that you are investigating. You will also be in a position to ask the **what if** questions. For example, **what** will happen to observation 3 **if** input 2 is removed. In many dissertation projects, establishing links can only be achieved by the application of statistical tools. Once you have a system that outputs large amounts of data then statistics must be used in its analysis.

TASK SCHEDULING

Having identified most of the tasks in your project, whether for a dissertation or thesis, you than have the difficult job of trying to attach execution times to each of them. In effect you need to generate a **Gantt Chart**. You and your supervisors will be able to use the Gantt Chart to monitor your progress. Quite possibly you will have to amend it from time to time as unforeseen difficulties occur. You must also remember that pursuing research is very much a time management exercise and to help you with the scheduling there are several software packages for the PC which are available. **Microsoft Project for Windows** is one example.

LAYOUT OF DISSERTATION OR THESIS

Once you have completed the work for your dissertation (or thesis) you are faced with the unenviable task of writing it up. It's a fact of life that you may put a great deal of work into writing your dissertation and only three people may read it apart from yourself: your proofreader, your supervisor and the external examiner.

After it has been examined and hopefully passed, a copy of it will find a place in the university's library and probably will never see the light of day again. If it's a research thesis, the British Library will make a microfiche of it. This will be stored in its vast bowels again with an equally ignominious future. If you have an industrial or commercial sponsor, its readership might be a little broader. Whatever the case, always remember that the principal objective is to secure you a Master's degree.

The contents page

When deciding the layout of the dissertation it is useful to start with the contents page which will have the chapter headings. This will act as the skeleton for the work and will allow you to define the order of each chapter. Once you are satisfied with the order, you begin to add meat to each contents heading by including chapter sub-headings. By the time you have completed this task you should have defined a place in your dissertation or thesis for every subject you intend to discuss.

What to include and exclude

The key rule for structuring a dissertation is **coherence**. Each chapter must fit together like a jigsaw. The contents of the chapters must be relevant and must serve a purpose in your argument. Don't include material that interrupts the coherence of the structure and does nothing to further the significance of your findings.

Sometimes you may feel tempted to add padding to the dissertation if you think that you're not going to reach the suggested word count. This is a mistake, the external examiner will see straight through this stratagem and will penalise you for it.

Sometimes you will have material that doesn't fit neatly into any chapter but still needs to be referred to. You can include such material in an **appendix**, thus giving a sense of completeness without interrupting the coherence of the dissertation.

For more information on the structure of the thesis, consult *Writing Your Dissertation* by Derek Swetnam (see Further Reading).

Format

You will require a wordprocessor to write your dissertation or thesis. Using a typewriter is not advisable, especially these days with the availability of low-cost PCs.

A typical front page of the document is shown in Figure 8. When selecting a font, use only Times Roman or Arial (for headings). You should consult the postgraduate handbook of your university to ascertain the preferred format.

Binding

The majority of universities require that at least one copy of the dissertation or thesis should be cloth-bound (hard covers). When you submit your dissertation to the binders, make sure that your instructions are clear. There is usually a strict format for the printing

Dissertation Title (24 Font)

Author (22 Font)

(Qualifications – 14 Font)

A dissertation (or thesis) submitted in partial fulfilment of the requirements of the University of xxx for the degree of M.xx (14 Font)

Date (14 Font)

Fig. 8. A typical front page of a Master's dissertation or thesis.

on the cover and the spine of the document. Check this, and your spelling, before taking it to the binders.

ORAL EXAMINATION

If you are doing a research Master's degree you will most certainly have to undergo an oral exam by an external examiner. On submission of your thesis, a copy will be sent to the external examiner for their perusal. On an appointed day, you will be expected to defend your thesis in a face-to-face encounter, which can be quite an ordeal depending on the quality of the work in the thesis. Normally there will be two examiners, an internal examiner, usually a member of the teaching staff, and the external. The session can last from as little as 40 minutes up to a few hours.

The external examiner

How well the exam goes will depend on the external examiner. They will have a list of questions for you to answer, usually referring to aspects of the thesis that were unclear and need clarifying. At the end of the exam, you will be asked to leave for a few minutes while the examiners deliberate. On re-entering the examination room you will be given the decision of the examiners. There are usually four options:

- recommendation of the award without corrections

- recommendation of the award on condition that corrections are carried out

- deferred, meaning that you are allowed to resubmit after you have done more work on your project

- fail.

The second option usually happens where the candidate has to correct typographical errors or make minor modifications to the thesis. Occasionally the third option is chosen, when the examiners feel that there is insufficient material in the thesis to merit the award of the degree, but the deficiency could be rectified by more work. It is very rare that the last option occurs. The candidate's supervisor should never have allowed the thesis to be submitted for this result to occur. Having said this, it does happen.

Preparing yourself for the oral exam

The only way you can prepare yourself for the oral exam is to read through the thesis a number of times and make sure that you are wholly familiar with its contents. Ask to discuss it with your supervisor.

Oral exams on taught Master's degrees

It's not usual for candidates on taught Master's degrees to have an oral exam, although this does happen on occasions, namely if the candidate is borderline on a fail or borderline on a distinction. If you are called for one, you will be told which is applicable to you.

If a candidate fails to satisfy the examiners with his/her dissertation, two options are usually available:

- The candidate can resubmit the dissertation after pursuing further work and rewriting part (or all) of it.

- The candidate can accept a Postgraduate Diploma (Pg.D.) or Certificate (Pg.C.) award from the university.

FINAL THOUGHTS

Having come thus far, you should be aware of the options open to you and what is expected of you in order to secure a Master's degree. Although it will involve a fair amount of hard work and application the rewards of having a Master's degree under your belt will more than compensate your efforts. As in many aspects of life, the more you put into it, the more you'll derive from it.

CHECKLIST

- Find out from your supervisor whether there is a document setting out the expected format for a project proposal. If not, discuss with them what they expect to see in the proposal.

- During the writing of your proposal, make a careful assessment of the resources required for your project.

- Make sure that you understand the regulations relating to the style, format and layout of the dissertation or thesis.

- On a taught Master's programme, you will have an expected submission date for the dissertation. Make sure that you include in your own schedule the time your dissertation will spend at the binders.

CASE STUDIES

Looking at an M.Sc. in environmental management

John works for a water company and has been pursuing a part-time Master's programme in environmental management. He's asked his manager for project suggestions which may be of interest to the company. His manager has given him several ideas.

John is in a very fortunate position, because he's been given a selection of projects from his employer, from which he has to choose one to work on. However, John's needs may very easily be at variance with his company's. John needs the project to secure his Master's degree. The projects from his manager relate to needs within the water company and the timescales may be quite unrealistic. John's course of action should include:

- A discussion with his supervisor on each of the suggested projects. John's supervisor will be in a position to evaluate the viability and suitability of each option.

- A realistic appraisal of whether he has sufficient knowledge and time to do justice to the selected project.

- An evaluation of the resources needed to pursue the chosen one and whether his company will provide them for him.

Using an M.Phil. for retraining in statistics

Alan is a biochemist working for a pharmaceutical company and has been edging towards a career in clinical testing. However, he needs a part-time retraining programme and has been thinking about a research M.Phil. in medical statistics.

There are a number of issues that Alan must resolve before he embarks on this type of programme.

- Is there a university within easy travelling distance where he can find a supervisor with sufficient expertise?

- Will his proposed research training programme be adequate to allow him to move into clinical testing? This information will be available from his line manager or a senior manager in the clinical testing division of his company.

- What would be the advantages of pursuing a taught Master's degree in medical statistics?

DISCUSSION POINTS

During the project period of your Master's programme you should keep in constant contact with your supervisor and discuss the following:

1. How much time is required for successful completion of the project, including the writing up time?

2. What resources are you likely to require? If additional resources are needed, such as equipment, will the university buy them for you?

3. If you are a part-time student, is it in your interest to find a project that is relevant to the needs of your employer? Discuss this possibility with your line manager.

4. What are your computer software requirements? Will the university fund any special packages you may need?

Appendix A:
British Institutions Running
Master's Degree Programmes

Here is a list of many of Britain's universities and colleges that run Master's degree programmes. To find out more, telephone the institution, ask for the higher degree office and request a postgraduate prospectus.

Aberdeen University. Tel: (0122) 427 3504.
Abertay Dundee University. Tel: (01382) 308080.
Anglia Polytechnic University. Tel: (01223) 363271.
Aston University. Tel: (0121) 359 6313.
Bath University. Tel: (01225) 826826.
Birmingham University. Tel: (0121) 414 3344.
Bolton College of Higher Education. Tel: (01204) 528851.
Bournemouth University. Tel: (01202) 524111.
Bradford University. Tel: (01274) 733466.
Brighton University. Tel: (01273) 600900.
Bristol University. Tel: (0117) 928 9000.
Bristol, West of England University. Tel: (0117) 965 6261.
Brunel University. Tel: (01895) 274000.
Buckingham University. Tel: (01280) 814080.
Cambridge University. Tel: (01223) 337733.
Canterbury (Kent) University. Tel: (01227) 782422.
Central England University. Tel: (0121) 331 5000.
Central Lancashire University. Tel: (01772) 201201.
Cheltenham & Gloucester College of Higher Education. Tel: (01242) 532700.
City University. Tel: (0171) 477 8000.
Coventry University. Tel: (01203) 631313.
Cranfield University. Tel: (01234) 750111.
De Montfort University. Tel: (0116) 255 1551.
Derby University. Tel: (01332) 622222.
Dundee University. Tel: (0138) 344028.
Durham University. Tel: (0191) 374 2000.

East Anglia University. Tel: (01603) 456161.
East London University. Tel: (0181) 590 7722.
Edinburgh University. Tel: (0131) 650 1000.
Essex University. Tel: (01206) 873666.
Exeter University. Tel: (01392) 263035.
Glamorgan University. Tel: (01443) 480480.
Glasgow University. Tel: (0141) 330 8855.
Glasgow Caledonian University. Tel: (0141) 331 3000.
Greenwich University. Tel: (0181) 331 8590.
Heriot-Watt University. Tel: (0131) 449 5111.
Hertfordshire University. Tel: (01707) 284000
Huddersfield University. Tel: (01484) 422288.
Hull University. Tel: (01482) 46311.
Humberside University. Tel: (01482) 440550.
Keele University. Tel: (01782) 621111.
Kent at Canterbury University. Tel: (01227) 764000.
Kingston University. Tel: (0181) 547 2000.
Lancaster University. Tel: (01524) 65201.
Leeds University. Tel: (0113) 233 2332.
Leeds Metropolitan University. Tel: (0113) 283 2600.
Leicester University. Tel: (0116) 252 2522.
Liverpool University. Tel: (0151) 794 2000.
Liverpool John Moores University. Tel: (0151) 231 2121.
London: Goldsmiths College. Tel: (0171) 919 7000.
London: Guildhall. Tel: (0171) 320 1000.
London: Imperial College. Tel: (0171) 589 5111.
London: Kings College. Tel: (0171) 836 5454.
London: LSE. Tel: (0171) 405 7686.
London: Queen Mary. Tel: (0171) 975 5555.
London: Royal Holloway. Tel: (01784) 434455.
London: University College. Tel: (0171) 387 7050.
Loughborough University. Tel: (01508) 263171.
Luton University. Tel: (01582) 34111.
Manchester University. Tel: (0161) 275 2077.
Manchester Metropolitan University. Tel: (0161) 247 2000.
Middlesex University. Tel: (0181) 362 5000.
Napier University. Tel: (0131) 444 2266.
Nene College. Tel: (01604) 735500.
Newcastle University. Tel: (0191) 222 6139.
North London University. Tel: (0171) 607 2789.
Northumbria University. Tel: (0191) 232 6002.
Nottingham University. Tel: (0115) 951 5151.

Nottingham Trent University. Tel: (0115) 941 8418.
Open University. Tel: (01908) 653231.
Oxford University. Tel: (01865) 270207.
Oxford Brooks University. Tel: (01865) 74111.
Paisley University. Tel: (0141) 848 3697.
Plymouth University. Tel: (01752) 600600.
Portsmouth University. Tel: (01705) 876543.
Queen's Belfast University. Tel: (01232) 245133.
Reading University. Tel: (01734) 875123.
Robert Gordon University. Tel: (01224) 262000.
Salford University. Tel: (0161) 754 5000.
Sheffield University. Tel: (0114) 276 8555.
Sheffield Hallam University. Tel: (0114) 272 0911.
Southampton University. Tel: (01703) 593712.
Southampton Institute. Tel: (01703) 319000.
South Bank University. Tel: (0171) 928 8989.
Staffordshire University. Tel: (01782) 294000.
St Andrews University. Tel: (01334) 426150.
Stirling University. Tel: (01786) 473171.
Strathclyde University. Tel: (0141) 553 4170.
Suffolk College. Tel: (01473) 255885.
Sunderland University. Tel: (0191) 510 9191.
Surrey University. Tel: (01483) 300800.
Sussex University. Tel: (01273) 678416.
Teeside University. Tel: (01642) 218121.
Thames Valley University. Tel: (0181) 231 2902.
Ulster University. Tel: (01265) 44141.
UMIST. Tel: (0161) 236 3311.
Wales: Aberystwyth. Tel: (01970) 622021.
Wales: Bangor. Tel: (01248) 351151.
Wales: Cardiff. Tel: (01222) 874404.
Wales: Lampeter. Tel: (01570) 422351.
Wales: Swansea. Tel: (01792) 205678.
Warwick University. Tel: (01203) 523523.
Westminster University. Tel: (0171) 911 5000.
Wolverhampton University. Tel: (01902) 321000.
York University. Tel: (0190) 443 0000.

Appendix B:
Institutions Sponsoring
Postgraduate Programmes

Agricultural Science and Economics: Ministry of Agriculture, Fisheries and Food. Tel: (0171) 238 5598.

Astronomy: Particle Physics and Astronomy Research Council (PRARC). Tel: (01793) 442026.

Biomedical: Medical Research Council (MRC). Tel: (0171) 636 5422.

Biotechnology and Biology: Biotechnology and Biological Sciences Research Council (BBSRC). Tel: (01793) 413200.

Economics: Economic and Social Research Council (ESRC). Tel: (01793) 413028.

Engineering: Engineering and Physical Sciences Research Council (EPSRC). Tel: (01793) 444308.

Geology: Natural Environment Research Council (NERC). Tel: (01793) 411562.

Humanities: The British Academy (BA). Tel: (0181) 951 5188.

Live Sciences: *see* Geology.

Medicine: *see* Biomedical.

Particle Physics: *see* Astronomy.

Social Science: *see* Economics.

Technology: *see* Engineering.

Glossary

Academic journals. When new information has been discovered or established from research, it's customary for the authors of the work to publish their findings in academic journals. Every academic subject has several journals which specialise in publishing research findings relating to the subject. Within a subject area, some journals are more prestigious than others.

Application form. When you apply for a Master's degree you will be expected to complete an application form. Great care should be taken when filling in this form. If there is considerable competition for places the first weeding out process will be the application form. If you are applying for a research M.Phil., the contents of the application form will be critical.

Assessment methods. Whatever course you pursue, there will be means of assessing your ability and progress. On a Master's programme these can include written examinations, assignments, laboratory work, presentations, oral examinations, seminar performance and a dissertation.

Assignments. One of the assessment methods which is commonly used in universities these days is the written assignment. Most assignments comprise a multi-part question which requires the student to perform background reading and searching for material. Each module will have at least one assignment which has to be prepared using a wordprocessor.

Bursaries. Many Master's degree programmes will have sponsors (usually research councils) who provide a minimum amount for a full-time postgraduate student to live on during the year they are pursuing a Master's degree. In general the number of bursaries attached to a Master's degree course is limited.

CD-ROM. The compact disc ROM is becoming a major storage medium for all types of information, irrespective of the subject area. All new PCs come with a CD-ROM drive.

Citation indices. Every paper published in an academic journal has references at the end of it – normally referring the reader to previous publications. A citation index lists all the publications that have referenced a published paper.

Dissertation. When pursuing a taught Master's degree, it's common practice for the university's regulations to require each candidate to work on a project of some sort. A description and the results of the project's execution are written up into a dissertation and submitted at the end of the course. The dissertation forms a major part of the assessment scheme.

Distance learning. An alternative means of pursuing a Master's programme is through distance learning (DL). DL is applicable to candidates who do not live within easy travelling distance of their chosen university or are unable to attend day-release courses. All the study material is sent out, by post, to the candidate, who is set deadlines for its completion.

Doctor of Philosophy (Ph.D.). Once a candidate has satisfied the requirements for a research M.Phil. degree, it's sometimes possible to transfer his/her registration to a Ph.D. degree. More work is required before a Ph.D. can be awarded which usually requires an **original contribution to knowledge.**

Employment support. Many part-time postgraduate students pursuing Master's degrees are able to secure support funding from their employer. This is particularly common if the student is conducting a project which is immediately relevant to the employer.

Examinations. Still regarded as one of the main assessment techniques, although in recent years emphasis has been shifting to other assessment methods. Performing well in exams requires practice.

External examiner. When the Master's degree has come to an end and all the assessment material has been submitted, the university will employ the services of an external examiner – usually a lecturer from another university. Their function is to ensure that standards are maintained and the assessment schemes are fair and have been carried out in a professional manner.

Full-time. When pursuing a full-time Master's degree a candidate will be expected to be available five days a week to attend all the timetabled events. It is customary for a full-time taught Master's degree to be completed within one calendar year.

Information databases. With the advent of information technology there has been an explosive growth of databases which carry vast amounts of information. Much of this information is of value to Master's degree students when pursuing the project research.

Investigation. One of the key processes in a Master's degree programme. Once a problem has been set, part of the task will be to ask questions, to review what is known, to unearth new information and consider it in the light of what is known. The idea is to develop an open mind and once open, broaden it.

Laboratory logbook. When pursuing a Master's degree that requires laboratory practice it's vitally important to keep a logbook of everything you do in the lab. Never rely on your memory, it's not as good as you think it is. Keeping a logbook is a very valuable exercise; after all, if you are prepared to invest your time, and sometimes money, to gain knowledge you should log that knowledge as it happens.

Lectures. The principal means of disseminating information in a university environment. Since they are timetabled, lectures enforce a discipline which is often to the student's benefit – a lecture is a work experience.

Library. Every university has a library and it should be considered as the principal resource to facilitate the learning experience. Candidates pursuing Master's programmes will be encouraged to use the library to seek out information.

MBA. Now regarded as an essential qualification for anyone pursuing a career in management, the Master of Business Administration degree has proved to be very popular, but is also very expensive in comparison to other Master's degree courses.

Modular system. The majority of universities in the UK have a modular system where all the material relating to a subject area is delivered in one term. At the end of the term, each student's assessment, for the module, is completed before the start of the new term. Credit is then given for the successful completion of a module. On some taught Master's degree courses, each candidate is expected to gain 180 credits, 60 credits from the dissertation and 120 credits from taught modules.

M.Phil. research. When pursuing a Master's degree through research it's customary for a candidate to register on an M. Phil. research programme. It does not have formal lectures but the learning programme is usually a tutorial format with the candidate's supervisor. The principal means of assessment is the thesis, submitted at the end of the research period.

New universities. In the early 1990s all the former polytechnics in the UK were reclassified as universities, awarding degrees in their own right.

Online service. It's now common practice to use a PC with a modem to access what are known as online services, whether they are commercial databases or services provided by Internet Service Providers (ISPs). These can be used as sources of information and are useful when seeking project information.

Oral examination. On submission of a thesis or dissertation it is customary for the Master's degree candidate to have an oral exam where they will be questioned by the external examiner on the nature of the work carried out for the thesis. Oral exams form part of the assessment procedure.

Part-time. One of the delivery modes of a Master's degree programme is part-time. Each candidate on the course is expected to spend some time every week (either a full day or a half day) attending lectures and tutorials at their university. Part-time Master's programmes usually take two years to complete.

Postgraduate diploma. To be awarded a Master's degree, each candidate is expected to gain sufficient credit in the normal assessment methods and a pass in the dissertation. If a candidate fails to submit a dissertation or fails the dissertation it's quite possible for the university to award a Postgraduate Diploma (Pg.D.) or Postgraduate Certificate (Pg.C.).

Postgraduate prospectus. Every university publishes a catalogue of the Master's degrees on offer. Known as the postgraduate prospectus, it contains information relating to the courses run by the university and is obtained by request from the higher degrees office.

Project supervisor. When you embark on a project, whether a taught Master's or a research M.Phil., you will be assigned a supervisor who will be knowledgeable in the area of the project. The role of the supervisor is to guide and supervise your project work.

Regulations. Every university has a set of regulations relating to the administration and execution of each Master's degree programme. When you register for a higher degree you will be issued with a set of regulations which state what conditions must be satisfied to be awarded a Master's degree. The regulations also contain information relating to the resolution of problems which might arise during the course of the programmes.

Research. When presented with a project idea, you will be expected to review, investigate, discover, analyse and arrive at conclusions. All these processes form part of the research procedure. When performed at a high level the research is expected to reveal new information, something that was not realised before. Conducting research requires thoroughness, patience and attention to detail.

Self-development. Much of the learning process on a Master's degree programme, whatever the mode of delivery, will result in self-development. The whole process of gaining new knowledge, learning how to apply it, and to analyse or solve problems, contributes to self-development.

Self-help groups. When working on a Master's programme run in the distance learning mode, a candidate is expected to become a member of a self-help group made up of other students, who live in the area, doing the same course. This provides an opportunity to share ideas and discuss difficulties.

Seminars. In many Master's degree programmes discussion is strongly encouraged and one effective means of achieving this is for the lecturer to have a series of topics. Each member of the class is asked to prepare a talk on one of the topics and present a seminar on it. The seminar takes the form of a talk followed by a group discussion on the issues raised in the talk.

Study material. Although lectures and tutorials play a major part in any Master's programme, every student will be expected to work on study material in their own time. Study material may take the form of references to books or articles or may be provided by the lecturer for private study.

Thesis project. When pursuing a research M.Phil. it is customary to have a project on which to conduct research. A thesis project is the means by which a candidate develops their research skills under the guidance of their supervisor. On completion of the research, the material is written up into a thesis and submitted for examination.

Tutorials. One of the principal means of learning from a tutor. Usually a small group of students meet every week for half an hour to an hour to discuss the issues covered in the week. Areas of uncertainty are discussed, giving an opportunity for the students to question material that needs clarifying.

Vivas. These are generally short (half an hour) interviews which take place between a student and two or more lecturers. The purpose of the viva is to enable the lecturers to ascertain the progress the student is making, or not making, whatever the case may be.

Further Reading

Buying a Personal Computer, Allen Brown (How To Books 1996)

How To Get a PhD: A Handbook for Students and their Supervisors, Estelle M. Phillips and D. S. Pugh (2nd edition, Open University Press 1995)

How To Pass Exams Without Anxiety, David Acres (4th edition, How To Books 1995)

Lateral Thinking, Edward De Bono (Penguin 1980)

Research Methods, Peter Marshall (How To Books 1997)

The Speed Reading Book, Tony Buzan (BBC Publications 1997)

Writing an Assignment, Pauline Smith (3rd edition, How To Books 1997)

Writing Your Dissertation, Derek Swetnam (2nd edition, How To Books 1997)

MBAs

The AMBA Guide to Business Schools (Tel: (0171) 837 3375)

The MBA Career Guide (Tel: (0171) 284 2641)

Which MBA? G. Bickerstaffe (ed) (EIB. Tel: (0171) 830 1007)

Index

GETTING THAT JOB
The complete job finders handbook

Joan Fletcher

Now in its fourth edition this popular book provides a clear step-by-step guide to identifying job opportunities, writing successful application letters, preparing for interviews and being selected. 'A valuable book.' *Teachers Weekly.* 'Cheerful and appropriate . . . particularly helpful in providing checklists designed to bring system to searching for a job. This relaxed, friendly and very helpful little book could bring lasting benefit.' *Times Educational Supplement.* 'Clear and concise . . . should be mandatory reading by all trainees.' *Comlon Magazine* (*LCCI*). Joan Fletcher is an experienced Manager and Student Counsellor.

128pp. illus. 1 85703 380 9. 4th edition.

HOW TO GET A JOB ABROAD
A handbook of opportunities and contacts

Roger Jones

Now in a fourth fully revised edition, this top-selling title is essential for everyone planning to spend a period abroad. It contains a big reference section of medium and long-term job opportunities and possibilities, arranged by region and country of the world, and by profession/ occupation. There are more than 100 pages of specific contacts and leads, giving literally hundreds of updated addresses and much hard-to-find information. There is a classified guide to overseas recruitment agencies, and even a multi-lingual guide to writing application letters. 'A fine book for anyone considering even a temporary overseas job.' *The Evening Star.* 'A highly informative and well researched book . . . containing lots of hard information and a first class reference section . . . A superb buy.' *The Escape Committee Newsletter.* 'A valuable addition to any careers library.' *Phoenix* (*Association of Graduate Careers Advisory Services*). 'An excellent addition to any careers library . . . Compact and realistic . . . There is a wide range of reference addresses covering employment agencies, specialist newspapers, a comprehensive booklist and helpful addresses . . . All readers, whether careers officers, young adults or more mature adults, will find use for this book.' *Newscheck/Careers Service Bulletin.* Roger Jones has himself worked abroad for many years and is a specialist writer on expatriate and employment matters.

272pp. illus. 1 85703 182 2. 4th edition.

HOW TO STUDY ABROAD
Your guide to successful planning and decision making

Teresa Tinsley

Studying abroad can open up a whole new horizon of opportunities, but what courses are available? How does one qualify? What does it cost? Can anyone do it? Now in a fully updated third edition, this book brings together a wealth of fascinating advice and reference information. It covers what to study (everything from short study visits to postgraduate opportunities), getting a place, entrance requirements, when and how to apply, grants and scholarships, helpful agencies and contacts, validation of courses, what to expect (teaching, services), financing your stay, accommodation, fitting in, travel and visas, health and insurance and more, and complete with a country-by-country guide. 'This book is straightforward to use, with a good index, lists all the main reference sources likely to be found in a careers library, and is just the thing to provide a quick answer to those difficult questions.' *Pheonix/ Association of Graduate Careers Advisory Services.* Teresa Tinsley BA DipEd MIL is Conferences Organiser at CILT, the Centre for Information on Language Teaching.

176pp. illus. 1 85703 169 5. 3rd edition.

APPLYING FOR A JOB
How to sell your skills and experience to a prospective employer

Judith Johnstone

Tough new realities have hit the jobs market. It is no longer enough to send employers mass-produced letters and CVs with vague details of 'hobbies and interests'. Employers want to know: 'What skills have you? How much personal commitment? Will it be worth training you longer term?' Whether you are a school or college leaver, a mature returner, out of work or facing redundancy, this book shows you step-by-step how to tackle job applications, how to decide what you are really offering, and how to sell this effectively to your future employer. 'Very practical and informative.' *Phoenix/Association of Graduate Careers Advisory Services.* Judith Johnstone is a qualified local government administrator and Member of the Institute of Personnel & Training. She has written extensively on employment topics.

160pp. illus. 1 85703 325 6. 3rd edition.

CAREER PLANNING FOR WOMEN
How to make a positive impact on your working life

Laurel Alexander

More women are entering the workplace than ever before. Whether it is on the corporate ladder or self employed, women are establishing a much stronger place for themselves within the world of commerce and industry. As global and national markets shift and business ethos develops, the specific qualities of women play a vital part alongside those of men. Business has been influenced primarily by male thought and action. Now there is the opportunity for women to make a substantial contribution with new ideas and approaches. The book is not about women taking men's jobs or about women being better or worse than men. It is intended to help women understand their unique and emerging role in business, change their perception of themselves and take much more responsibility for their responses and actions within the workplace. Laurel Alexander is a manager/trainer in career development who has helped many individuals succeed in changing their work direction. She is also author of *Surviving Redundancy* in this series.

160pp. illus. 1 85703 417 1.

SPENDING A YEAR ABROAD
How to have the time of your life anywhere around the world

Nick Vandome

A year abroad is now a very popular option among thousands of school leavers, students, and people taking a mid-life break. This book sets out the numerous options available from making the decision to go, to working on a kibbutz, to teaching English as a foreign language, to adapting to life at home on your return. 'Should be required reading . . . Unlike most reference books this is one which should be read right through, and that is a pleasure as well as being very informative. It is totally comprehensive . . . very good value for money.' *The School Librarian*. 'Excellent.' *Careers Guidance Today*. Nick Vandome is a young freelance writer who has spent a year abroad on three occasions, in France, Australia, Africa and Asia. His articles have appeared in *The Guardian*, *The Scotsman*, *The Daily Telegraph*, and elsewhere.

176pp illus. 1 85703 459 7. 3rd edition.

WRITING YOUR DISSERTATION
How to plan, prepare and present your work successfully

Derek Swetnam

Almost all advanced educational courses now include a dissertation or research project of some type. For many students this can be a terrifying experience as the time for submission approaches and tutors are elusive. Although colleges and universities may have different systems, basic principles for planning research and making the inevitable compromise between what is desirable and what is feasible are the same. Some mature students may not have written extensively for years but it is assumed that they can cope with minimum help. This new book offers a plain guide to ways of producing an excellent dissertation with minimum stress and frustration. It covers choosing a subject, planning the total work, selecting research methods and techniques, written style and presentation. The author is a former Course Leader of a large Master's level programme at the Manchester Metropolitan University.

102pp. illus. 1 85703 445 7. 2nd edition.

HOW TO MASTER LANGUAGES
For business, study, travel and living abroad

Roger Jones

With the expansion of international contacts and the advent of the global market, languages are more valuable than ever before. Written for business people, students and others, this book discusses: why learn a language, which language to choose, language training and where to find it, getting down to language learning, children and languages, and language training in organisations. A large reference section completes this book, giving information on an enormous variety of courses, guides and study material, providing an overview of the world's myriad languages and their use today. 'Full of really practical information and advice, this book will show you how to make the right choices, and add a whole new dimension to your social life, career and business prospects.' *Nexus Expatriate Magazine*. Roger Jones DipTESL is himself an experienced linguist, writer and educational consultant.

160pp. illus. 1 85703 092 3.

How To Books provide practical help on a large range of topics. They are available through all good bookshops or can be ordered direct from the distributors. Just tick the titles you want and complete the form on the following page.

- ___ Apply to an Industrial Tribunal (£7.99)
- ___ Applying for a Job (£8.99)
- ___ Applying for a United States Visa (£15.99)
- ___ Backpacking Round Europe (£8.99)
- ___ Be a Freelance Journalist (£8.99)
- ___ Be a Freelance Secretary (£8.99)
- ___ Become a Freelance Sales Agent (£9.99)
- ___ Become an Au Pair (£8.99)
- ___ Becoming a Father (£8.99)
- ___ Buy & Run a Shop (£8.99)
- ___ Buy & Run a Small Hotel (£8.99)
- ___ Buying a Personal Computer (£9.99)
- ___ Career Networking (£8.99)
- ___ Career Planning for Women (£8.99)
- ___ Cash from your Computer (£9.99)
- ___ Choosing a Nursing Home (£9.99)
- ___ Choosing a Package Holiday (£8.99)
- ___ Claim State Benefits (£9.99)
- ___ Collecting a Debt (£9.99)
- ___ Communicate at Work (£7.99)
- ___ Conduct Staff Appraisals (£7.99)
- ___ Conducting Effective Interviews (£8.99)
- ___ Coping with Self Assessment (£9.99)
- ___ Copyright & Law for Writers (£8.99)
- ___ Counsel People at Work (£7.99)
- ___ Creating a Twist in the Tale (£8.99)
- ___ Creative Writing (£9.99)
- ___ Critical Thinking for Students (£8.99)
- ___ Dealing with a Death in the Family (£9.99)
- ___ Do Voluntary Work Abroad (£8.99)
- ___ Do Your Own Advertising (£8.99)
- ___ Do Your Own PR (£8.99)
- ___ Doing Business Abroad (£10.99)
- ___ Doing Business on the Internet (£12.99)
- ___ Emigrate (£9.99)
- ___ Employ & Manage Staff (£8.99)
- ___ Find Temporary Work Abroad (£8.99)
- ___ Finding a Job in Canada (£9.99)
- ___ Finding a Job in Computers (£8.99)
- ___ Finding a Job in New Zealand (£9.99)
- ___ Finding a Job with a Future (£8.99)
- ___ Finding Work Overseas (£9.99)
- ___ Freelance DJ-ing (£8.99)
- ___ Freelance Teaching & Tutoring (£9.99)
- ___ Get a Job Abroad (£10.99)
- ___ Get a Job in America (£9.99)
- ___ Get a Job in Australia (£9.99)
- ___ Get a Job in Europe (£9.99)
- ___ Get a Job in France (£9.99)
- ___ Get a Job in Travel & Tourism (£8.99)
- ___ Get into Radio (£8.99)
- ___ Getting into Films & Television (£10.99)
- ___ Getting That Job (£8.99)
- ___ Getting your First Job (£8.99)
- ___ Going to University (£8.99)
- ___ Helping your Child to Read (£8.99)
- ___ How to Study & Learn (£8.99)
- ___ Investing in People (£9.99)
- ___ Investing in Stocks & Shares (£9.99)
- ___ Keep Business Accounts (£7.99)
- ___ Know Your Rights at Work (£8.99)
- ___ Live & Work in America (£9.99)
- ___ Live & Work in Australia (£12.99)
- ___ Live & Work in Germany (£9.99)
- ___ Live & Work in Greece (£9.99)
- ___ Live & Work in Italy (£8.99)
- ___ Live & Work in New Zealand (£9.99)
- ___ Live & Work in Portugal (£9.99)
- ___ Live & Work in the Gulf (£9.99)
- ___ Living & Working in Britain (£8.99)
- ___ Living & Working in China (£9.99)
- ___ Living & Working in Hong Kong (£10.99)
- ___ Living & Working in Israel (£10.99)
- ___ Living & Working in Saudi Arabia (£12.99)
- ___ Living & Working in the Netherlands (£9.99)
- ___ Making a Complaint (£8.99)
- ___ Making a Wedding Speech (£8.99)
- ___ Manage a Sales Team (£8.99)
- ___ Manage an Office (£8.99)
- ___ Manage Computers at Work (£8.99)
- ___ Manage People at Work (£8.99)
- ___ Manage Your Career (£8.99)
- ___ Managing Budgets & Cash Flows (£9.99)
- ___ Managing Meetings (£8.99)
- ___ Managing Your Personal Finances (£8.99)
- ___ Managing Yourself (£8.99)
- ___ Market Yourself (£8.99)
- ___ Master Book-Keeping (£8.99)
- ___ Mastering Business English (£8.99)
- ___ Master GCSE Accounts (£8.99)
- ___ Master Public Speaking (£8.99)
- ___ Migrating to Canada (£12.99)
- ___ Obtaining Visas & Work Permits (£9.99)
- ___ Organising Effective Training (£9.99)
- ___ Pass Exams Without Anxiety (£7.99)
- ___ Passing That Interview (£8.99)
- ___ Plan a Wedding (£7.99)
- ___ Planning Your Gap Year (£8.99)
- ___ Prepare a Business Plan (£8.99)
- ___ Publish a Book (£9.99)
- ___ Publish a Newsletter (£9.99)
- ___ Raise Funds & Sponsorship (£7.99)
- ___ Rent & Buy Property in France (£9.99)
- ___ Rent & Buy Property in Italy (£9.99)

How To Books

___ Research Methods (£8.99)	___ Use the Internet (£9.99)
___ Retire Abroad (£8.99)	___ Winning Consumer Competitions (£8.99)
___ Return to Work (£7.99)	___ Winning Presentations (£8.99)
___ Run a Voluntary Group (£8.99)	___ Work from Home (£8.99)
___ Setting up Home in Florida (£9.99)	___ Work in an Office (£7.99)
___ Spending a Year Abroad (£8.99)	___ Work in Retail (£8.99)
___ Start a Business from Home (£7.99)	___ Work with Dogs (£8.99)
___ Start a New Career (£6.99)	___ Working Abroad (£14.99)
___ Starting to Manage (£8.99)	___ Working as a Holiday Rep (£9.99)
___ Starting to Write (£8.99)	___ Working in Japan (£10.99)
___ Start Word Processing (£8.99)	___ Working in Photography (£8.99)
___ Start Your Own Business (£8.99)	___ Working in the Gulf (£10.99)
___ Study Abroad (£8.99)	___ Working in Hotels & Catering (£9.99)
___ Study & Live in Britain (£7.99)	___ Working on Contract Worldwide (£9.99)
___ Studying at University (£8.99)	___ Working on Cruise Ships (£9.99)
___ Studying for a Degree (£8.99)	___ Write a Press Release (£9.99)
___ Successful Grandparenting (£8.99)	___ Write a Report (£8.99)
___ Successful Mail Order Marketing (£9.99)	___ Write an Assignment (£8.99)
___ Successful Single Parenting (£8.99)	___ Write & Sell Computer Software (£9.99)
___ Survive Divorce (£8.99)	___ Write for Publication (£8.99)
___ Surviving Redundancy (£8.99)	___ Write for Television (£8.99)
___ Taking in Students (£8.99)	___ Writing a CV that Works (£8.99)
___ Taking on Staff (£8.99)	___ Writing a Non Fiction Book (£9.99)
___ Taking Your A-Levels (£8.99)	___ Writing an Essay (£8.99)
___ Teach Abroad (£8.99)	___ Writing & Publishing Poetry (£9.99)
___ Teach Adults (£8.99)	___ Writing & Selling a Novel (£8.99)
___ Teaching Someone to Drive (£8.99)	___ Writing Business Letters (£8.99)
___ Travel Round the World (£8.99)	___ Writing Reviews (£9.99)
___ Understand Finance at Work (£8.99)	___ Writing Your Dissertation (£8.99)
___ Use a Library (£7.99)	

To: Plymbridge Distributors Ltd, Plymbridge House, Estover Road, Plymouth PL6 7PZ. Customer Services Tel: (01752) 202301. Fax: (01752) 202331.

Please send me copies of the titles I have indicated. Please add postage & packing (UK £1, Europe including Eire, £2, World £3 airmail).

☐ I enclose cheque/PO payable to Plymbridge Distributors Ltd for £

☐ Please charge to my ☐ MasterCard, ☐ Visa, ☐ AMEX card.

Account No.

Card Expiry Date   19   ☎ Credit Card orders may be faxed or phoned.

Customer Name (CAPITALS) ....

Address ....

.... Postcode ....

Telephone .... Signature ....

Every effort will be made to despatch your copy as soon as possible but to avoid possible disappointment please allow up to 21 days for despatch time (42 days if overseas). Prices and availability are subject to change without notice.

Code BPA